that Special touch.

A
Cookbook
By
Sandra Davis

I am first and foremost a happy wife and a proud mother of two children. Because of that, I dedicate this book to my family:

Joe B., J. Ashley and Anne Nicole

They have shared the dream of this cookbook with me from its very beginning to its beautiful published form. Even more important, they have given me "a special touch" when I needed it.

I want to express my heartfelt appreciation to my extended family – especially my mother and grandmother, who taught me what hospitality, entertaining and good food are all about. I thank my friends and business associates who encouraged me throughout and never let my enthusiasm waver.

Many thanks to all of you. THAT SPECIAL TOUCH is for you!

Sandra

ACKNOWLEDGEMENTS

Special thanks to:

Bill Samuels, Jr., president, Maker's Mark Distillery and all employees of Maker's Mark for their enthusiasm and cooperation.

Maker's Mark is a registered trademark of Maker's Mark Distillery Inc. and is used with full permission.

Additional copies of THAT SPECIAL TOUCH may be ordered from:

Special Touch Publishing
P.O. Box 427
Springfield, KY 40069
(606) 336-7749
Fax # (606) 336-3960

Copyright © 1990 by Sandra Davis
Special Touch, Inc.
P.O. Box 427
124 East Main Street
Springfield, Kentucky 40069

First Printing, March, 1990
Printed in the United States of America

Library of Congress Catalog Card Number 89-92544
International Standard Book Number 0-9625232-0-8

Graphic Design by Perrone Mabry Phillips, Inc., Louisville, KY
Printing by Fetter Printing Company, Louisville, KY

TABLE OF CONTENTS

M aker's Mark bourbon and simply elegant recipes . . . what a perfect combination.

I was born a few miles from the quaint and unique Maker's Mark Distillery (featured in the photographs of this book), and I've been collecting, creating and refining Maker's-Mark-only recipes for more than 20 years.

Cooking with bourbon adds excitement to your dishes. It imparts a woody, nutty taste, and it's an easy way to turn a ho-hum recipe into something special that your guests will enjoy. And because Maker's Mark is handcrafted to be so smooth, the taste is never overpowering.

Of course, when you cook anything containing bourbon at 172 degrees (a low simmer) or higher, it loses its alcoholic content. If you want the spirits to linger, add bourbon last. Or, if you like the recipe but prefer to have it without bourbon, just add water, milk or fruit juice as a substitute.

Enjoy these recipes and remember. . . any recipe can be improvised to reflect the unique personality of the cook. That's what makes cooking so exciting. So be yourself! Cook from your heart with enthusiasm and inspiration, and you'll add your own special touch every time.

Sandra Davis

I f you had moved to Nelson County, Kentucky, in mid 1780 with a group of pioneers from Pennsylvania, one of your neighbors may have been Robert Samuels. And later on, in the early 1800's, you may have known some folks in Marion County named Burks, who emigrated to Kentucky from Maryland.

What these two families had in common was distilling. But it wasn't until 1953 that their paths crossed when Taylor William (Bill) Samuels Sr. bought the old Burks water-powered grist mill, and later a distillery, to realize his dream of making a special new sippin' whisky.

A sixth-generation distiller and direct descendent of Robert Samuels, T. W. Samuels Sr. was determined to make a better whisky than his family had ever made… and a better whisky than anybody else was making in 1953. He had his own ideas about how a quality bourbon should taste, and he started by burning the whisky recipe his family had used for more than 100 years.

Opposite side photo: (Left to right) Maker's On-the-Rocks, Hospitality-Filled Tomatoes, Bourbon Punch, Kentucky Mulled Cider, Special Mint Julep, Spiked Cranberry Cocktail, Holiday Cheese Ball, Bourbon-Orange Cooler

AMAZING PATÉ

Yields 2 cups

"Try it, you'll like it."

¼ lb. butter (1 stick)
1 onion, chopped
2 garlic cloves, chopped or
    ¼ tsp. garlic powder
1 (8-ounce) liverwurst, cut into
    chunks
2 Tbs. Maker's Mark
½ tsp. nutmeg
¼ tsp. allspice
Salt and pepper

- Melt the butter in a skillet, add onions, cover, and simmer about 10 minutes or until they are soft; do not allow them to brown. Add the rest of ingredients and cook mixture over brisk heat, stirring and breaking up liverwurst until it seems to have absorbed some of the butter; this should take 5–10 minutes.

- Transfer the contents of skillet to a blender or food processor and process till mixture is very smooth. Taste for seasonings and correct if necessary.

- Scrape puree into a 2-cup mold and chill; it's best if refrigerated for 2–3 days before serving.

MAKER'S PATÉ

Serves 8

"An old favorite recipe."

2 lbs. fresh chicken livers
1 medium-sized onion, grated
¾ C. salad dressing
1 Tbs. Maker's Mark
1 hard-cooked egg,
    chopped fine
Salt and pepper to taste

- Boil chicken livers in covered saucepan, medium heat, 10–15 minutes. Remove from heat, drain and cool.

- Chop livers finely, adding onions to livers.

- Put into medium-size mixing bowl of electric mixer, adding all other ingredients. Beat at medium speed for 10 minutes or until fluffy.

- Butter mold, fill with paté and place in refrigerator for several hours or overnight.

- Take out of refrigerator half hour before removing from mold. If necessary, place hot, wet towels on mold to help loosen paté.

- Serve with crackers.

VERY BOURBON FRUIT DIP

Yields 2½ cups

"This is the perfect dip for fresh strawberries."

½ C. brown sugar, melted
¼ C. Maker's Mark
2 C. sour cream
Powdered sugar

- In a small saucepan, melt the brown sugar with the bourbon; cool.

- Add sour cream, thicken with powdered sugar to desired consistency.

- Serve as dip for fresh fruit.

MUSHROOM DELIGHT

Serves 6

"It's one of those special dishes no one will forget!"

1 lb. mushrooms
3 Tbs. grated onion
3 Tbs. vegetable oil
1 jigger Maker's Mark
1 Tbs. lemon juice
Salt
Sour cream (½ C. or more)

■ Clean a pound of medium-sized mushrooms by dipping them individually in a mixture of 1 cup water and 2 tablespoons lemon juice, brushing them with a pastry brush. Remove the stems (save for soup!) and cut the caps into quarters.

■ Sauté them with grated onion and vegetable oil (not olive oil this time, it's too strong in flavor). Cook the mushrooms very gently and not too long—about 5 minutes.

■ Remove from heat, sprinkle lightly with salt and pour over them Maker's Mark and lemon juice.

■ Chill for several hours, turning once or twice to assure an even marinade. Before serving, mix lightly with sour cream and garnish with a sprinkle of fresh chives or parsley.

■ Enjoy with assorted crackers or as a side dish with beef.

"SPIRIT OF KENTUCKY" CHEESE BALL

Serves 12

"A cheese ball that combines lots of Kentucky flavors."

1 lb. butter
1 lb. Roquefort or bleu cheese
½ C. Maker's Mark
¼ C. sesame seeds

■ Cream butter and cheese with sesame seeds; add bourbon slowly.

■ Shape into a ball; refrigerate 24 hours.

■ Serve with crackers or beaten biscuits.

CREAMY ORANGE DIP

Yields 1¾ cups

"Always keep ingredients in pantry for this tasty dip."

1 (8-ounce) container soft
   cream cheese
1 (7-ounce) jar marshmallow
   cream
1 Tbs. grated orange rind
1 Tbs. frozen orange juice
   concentrate
1 Tbs. Maker's Mark
   (or to taste)

■ Combine cream cheese and marshmallow cream; beat until smooth.

■ Stir in remaining ingredients.

■ Cover and chill for 1–2 hours; serve with assorted fresh fruit.

CHEESE BOURBON FONDUE

Yields 2½ cups

*"A sprinkle of freshly ground pepper adds even more spice
to this cheese dip."*

3 Tbs. all-purpose flour
½ tsp. white pepper
⅛ tsp. ground nutmeg
3 C. (12 ounces) shredded Swiss
    cheese
1 C. (4 ounces) shredded
    Cheddar cheese
1 C. dry white wine
¼ C. Maker's Mark
2 lbs. assorted vegetables
    (boiled new potatoes,
    blanched cauliflowerets,
    broccoli flowerets, baby
    carrots, fresh mushrooms
    and radishes)
French bread cubes

- Combine flour, white pepper and nutmeg in a large bowl; add cheese to flour mixture, coating thoroughly. Set aside.
- Heat wine in a heavy saucepan over low heat until hot (do not boil); gradually stir cheese mixture into wine; cook over low heat until cheese melts and mixture thickens, stirring constantly. (Do not overcook or cheese will become stringy.)
- Remove from heat and gradually stir in bourbon.
- Pour mixture into a chafing dish or fondue pot over a low flame; serve with vegetables and bread cubes for dipping.

OYSTERS "LOUISVILLE"

Serves any number

"Men really love this spicy appetizer."

Raw oysters
Strips of bacon, cut in half
Sliced or halved water
    chestnuts
Maker's Mark Gourmet Sauce

- Wrap strip of bacon around an oyster with a piece of water chestnut in it, secure with toothpicks.
- Pour Gourmet Sauce over oysters and broil until bacon is cooked on one side, turn and broil other side.
- Serve hot.

CRANBERRY CHUTNEY AND CHEESE

Yields 4½ cups

"This chutney is also great as an accompaniment to any meat."

1 lb. (4 cups) fresh cranberries
2 Granny Smith apples, peeled,
    cored and diced
1 pear, peeled, cored and diced
1 C. golden raisins
¼ C. minced onion
1 C. sugar
1 Tbs. grated orange peel
1 tsp. ground cinnamon
⅛ tsp. freshly grated nutmeg
¼ C. fresh orange juice
3 Tbs. Maker's Mark

- In a heavy, 3-quart saucepan, combine all ingredients except bourbon.
- Bring to boil over high heat; reduce heat and simmer, uncovered, till thick, about 45 minutes, stirring occasionally.
- Stir in bourbon; cool and store leftover chutney in the refrigerator.
- Serve over cream cheese as instant appetizer or put in decorative jar for a quick hostess gift.

STUFFED MUSHROOMS

Yields 24

"This appetizer is best served straight from the oven."

24 whole medium-size
  mushrooms
1 C. butter, melted
2 small onions, chopped
3 garlic cloves, minced
½ C. minced parsley
2 Tbs. flour
½ C. seasoned bread crumbs
1 C. sour cream
Salt and pepper to taste
Maker's Mark
Freshly grated Parmesan
  cheese

- Remove and chop mushroom stems.
- In medium-size bowl combine chopped stems, butter, onions, garlic and parsley and mix well. Add flour, bread crumbs, sour cream, salt and pepper; blend well.
- Arrange mushroom caps—hollow side up—in a shallow baking dish. Drizzle a small amount of bourbon in each cap and then fill with stuffing. Sprinkle tops of mushrooms with Parmesan cheese.
- Add just enough Maker's Mark to cover bottom of baking dish; bake in a preheated 375° oven for 20 minutes.
- Serve hot.

HOSPITALITY-FILLED TOMATOES

Serves 20

"Everyone always asks for this recipe."

1 pt. cherry tomatoes
1 (4½-ounce) can deviled ham
2 Tbs. sour cream
2 Tbs. horseradish
1 tsp. Maker's Mark

- Early in day, slice thin tops from tomatoes; remove pulp and drain shells upside down on paper towels.
- In small bowl combine all other ingredients; fill tomatoes with mixture and refrigerate.
- Tomatoes are best when served the same day they are filled.

COCKTAIL CASSEROLE

Serves 8

"A must for a Christmas party."

1 (8-ounce) pkg. cream cheese
1 Tbs. Maker's Mark
6½ ounces of flaked crabmeat
2 tsp. minced onions
½ tsp. horseradish
¼ tsp. salt
Dash of pepper
1 tsp. Worcestershire sauce
Sliced almonds

- Blend all ingredients except almonds; put in an oven proof dish and sprinkle with sliced almonds.
- Bake for 15 minutes at 375°.
- Serve with toast rounds.

HOLIDAY CHEESE BALL

Yields 4¹/₂ cups

"Make this cheese ball using the cranberry chutney recipe in this book as an ingredient, and you'll have a double delight."

1 (8-ounce) pkg. cream cheese, softened
1 (8¹/₂-ounce) can crushed pineapple, drained
2 C. chopped pecans
¹/₄ C. chopped green pepper
3 Tbs. chopped onion
1 tsp. seasoned salt
2 Tbs. chopped chutney
1¹/₂ Tbs. Maker's Mark
Maraschino cherries
Parsley

- Beat cream cheese slightly; gradually stir in all other ingredients reserving 1 cup pecans to roll ball in and cherries and parsley for garnish.
- Chill well.
- Shape into ball and roll in remaining 1 cup pecans. Chill until serving time.
- Garnish with maraschino cherries and parsley and serve with assorted crackers.

SHRIMP BITES FLAMBÉ

Serves 10

"Worth the effort."

2 lbs. shelled raw shrimp
¹/₂ lb. sliced bacon
¹/₂ C. Maker's Mark

- Wrap each shrimp in a narrow strip of bacon; fasten with toothpick.
- Spread in shallow pan and bake in 450° oven, turning frequently until bacon is crisp; drain.
- Put into chafing dish; pour bourbon over shrimp and bacon. Ignite and serve immediately.

GOURMET SHRIMP CAKE

Serves 10

"This recipe is enhanced by the special Maker's Mark Gourmet Sauce."

11 ounces cream cheese, softened
1 Tbs. mayonnaise
2 Tbs. milk
1 (4-ounce) jar horseradish
Dash of Worcestershire sauce
2 (4¹/₂-ounces each) cans shrimp, chopped
1 C. Maker's Mark Gourmet Sauce

- Blend first three ingredients until smooth.
- Add remaining ingredients; blend well, pour into mold and freeze.
- Thaw before serving. Unmold and serve with crackers, adding a small amount of Gourmet Sauce to each serving.

BEEF BARBECUE CUPS

Serves 12

"This recipe uses the famous Maker's Mark Gourmet Sauce."

1 lb. sirloin, ground
½ C. Maker's Mark Gourmet
  Sauce
1 tsp. liquid brown sugar
1 tsp. mustard
1 tsp. Worcestershire sauce
1 tsp. minced onion
1 (8-ounce) can refrigerator
  biscuits
½ C. cheddar cheese

- Sauté ground sirloin until browned and crumbly; drain, stirring in Maker's Mark Gourmet Sauce, onion, brown sugar liquid, mustard and Worcestershire sauce.

- Place each biscuit in greased muffin cups; press to cover bottom and sides. Spoon mixture into cups and sprinkle with cheese.

- Bake at 400° for 10–12 minutes or until golden brown and serve immediately.

- If you don't have liquid brown sugar, dissolve dry brown sugar in 1 tablespoon water and sauté mixture a few minutes longer.

ESPRESSO PECANS

Yields 1½ cups

"Always gets compliments."

¼ C. sugar
2 Tbs. Maker's Mark
2 tsp. freeze-dried instant
  coffee
¼ tsp. cinnamon
1½ C. shelled pecans

- In large skillet, combine ingredients in order listed; bring to boil over medium heat, stirring constantly, until pecans are well glazed.

- Spread on waxed paper to cool.

- Serve or give as a hostess gift.

HOT TEA PUNCH

"Mix of bourbon, wine and spices add zip to this tea."

2 qts. water
3¼ C. Burgundy or other
   red wine
1 C. Maker's Mark
2 oranges, sliced
2 lemons, sliced
3 (3-inch) sticks cinnamon
1½ tsp. whole cloves
2 family-size tea bags
1½ C. sugar

- Combine first 7 ingredients in a large Dutch oven; bring to a boil. Remove from heat; add tea bags.
- Cover and let stand 5 minutes; remove tea bags.
- Add sugar; heat tea mixture just until the sugar dissolves, stirring occasionally.
- Serve hot.

MAKER'S ON-THE-ROCKS

Serves 1

"A Kentucky handcrafted drink."

2 or 3 ice cubes
1 jigger Maker's Mark
Lemon twist for garnish

- Just before serving, pour Maker's Mark over ice cubes in old-fashioned glass, add lemon twist. (With liquor, some people may request a dash of water.)
- Enjoy!

WARM ORANGE CIDER

Serves 16

"A delicious fireside drink."

1 (12-ounce) can frozen orange
   juice concentrate
1½ qts. apple cider
½ C. Maker's Mark
1 orange, cut into 12 slices

- Prepare orange juice as directed on can and heat with apple cider over low heat just to boiling.
- Pour 1 cup orange juice mixture into each mug; stir in 2 teaspoons bourbon and top with orange slice.
- Garnish with stick cinnamon if desired.

THE ORIGINAL HOT TODDY

Serves 1

"This drink has been prescribed for many years when a person has a cold—and needs a lift!"

½ tsp. sugar
2 whole cloves
1 small cinnamon stick
1 lemon slice
1 jigger Maker's Mark

- Measure into an old-fashioned glass all ingredients.
- Place teaspoon in glass; add boiling water to fill glass. (Teaspoon helps prevent glass from breaking when boiling water is added.)
- Stir mixture and serve immediately.

COCONOG
Yields 5 cups

"A tropical drink."

1 (13-ounce) can evaporated
   milk
1 (8½-ounce) can cream of
   coconut
½ C. Maker's Mark
1 C. white sugar
4 eggs
½ tsp. vanilla extract
Maraschino cherries (optional)

- Combine all ingredients in container of electric blender and process until smooth.
- Chill; serve in cups and garnish each serving with a maraschino cherry, if desired.

SPIKED COCOA
Yields 1 cup

"A great treat to enjoy on a winter night."

1 C. milk
1 tsp. hot chocolate mix
1 tsp. coffee creamer
1 tsp. Maker's Mark

- For each person, heat a cup of milk to steaming. Remove from heat before bubbles begin to form around edge of saucepan.
- Into cup or mug, measure chocolate mix, coffee creamer and bourbon. Add hot milk; stir until well mixed.
- Recipe can be easily increased to serve any number of people.

PICKLED PEACH SLUSH
Yields 1 large drink

"Bourbon and peaches—always a terrific combination."

½ overripe peach
1 heaping tsp. sugar
2 jiggers Maker's Mark
   (3 ounces)
Crushed ice

- Mash together peach and sugar, add Maker's Mark and stir well.
- Fill glass with crushed ice and serve.

BUTTERED LEMONADE
Yields 3¾ cups

"A lemonade that is served hot!"

½ C. sugar
¼ tsp. grated lemon rind
½ C. lemon juice
¼ C. Maker's Mark
3 C. water
1 Tbs. butter or margarine
Cinnamon sticks (optional)

- Combine all ingredients except cinnamon sticks in saucepan. Cook over medium heat until butter melts and mixture's hot.
- Serve with cinnamon stick stirrers, if desired.

FROZEN WHISKY SOURS

Serves 12

"Keep this mixture in freezer for spontaneous entertaining."

1 (6-ounce) can frozen
  lemonade concentrate
2½ cans Maker's Mark
  (use lemonade can for
  measuring)
1 can diluted orange juice
  (use lemonade can for
  measuring)
2 cans water (use lemonade
  can for measuring)

- Day before or several days ahead, combine all ingredients and freeze in plastic container. (Mixture does not freeze solid.)
- Just before serving, put portion of frozen mixture in blender and whirl until smooth and slushy.
- Pour into cocktail glass and garnish with cherry and half an orange slice.
- If you thaw mixture slightly, it's not necessary to use blender; just spoon into glasses.

BOURBON PUNCH

Serves 12

"This pink punch is perfect for any lazy summer afternoon."

1 (12-ounce) can pink
  lemonade, undiluted
1 (64-ounce) bottle 7-Up
1 jar maraschino cherries
1 C. Maker's Mark

- Mix all ingredients in large bowl.
- Freeze until ready to use.
- Serve slushy.

WHISKY FLIP

Serves 1

"A drink you will flip over."

1 egg
1 tsp. powdered sugar
1½ ounces Maker's Mark
2 tsp. sweet cream (optional)
Nutmeg

- Shake ingredients together well with some cracked ice, then strain into a 5-ounce flip glass.
- Grate a little nutmeg on top and serve.

MAKER'S FRUIT COOLER

Serves 6

"A drink with lots of spirit."

1 (6-ounce) can frozen
  pineapple juice concentrate
2 medium bananas peeled and
  cut into several pieces
1 C. ice cubes
2 Tbs. sugar
1½ C. club soda
⅔ C. Maker's Mark

- Combine frozen pineapple juice concentrate, bananas, ice cubes and sugar in processor or blender and mix until smooth.
- Transfer to chilled pitcher, stirring in club soda and Maker's Mark.
- Serve immediately.

BOURBON-CITRUS SLUSH

Serves 6

"Keep this punch stored in freezer for use anytime!"

2 tea bags
1 C. boiling water
1 C. sugar
1 (6-ounce) can frozen orange
 juice concentrate, thawed (⅔ C.)
½ C. Maker's Mark
½ of a (6-ounce) can frozen
 lemonade concentrate,
 thawed (⅓ C.)
3½ C. tap water

- Steep tea in boiling water for 2–3 minutes; remove tea bags and stir in sugar.
- Add remaining ingredients and 3½ cups water; mix till sugar is dissolved.
- Pour into container and freeze firm.
- Remove from freezer about 10 minutes before serving; spoon into cocktail glasses and garnish with lemon wedges, if desired.
- Keep unused portion in freezer.

KENTUCKY MULLED CIDER

Yields 8 cups

"A winter delight–allow 3 cups per guest."

1 C. Maker's Mark
4 C. cider
1 lemon
6 cloves
½ tsp. allspice (ground)
2 small sticks cinnamon

- Combine Maker's Mark and cider.
- Add 1 thinly sliced lemon with rind, cloves, allspice and sticks of cinnamon.
- Heat to boiling point and serve.
- *Hint*—For 100 guests, multiply recipe by 35, converting liquids to quarts.

STRAWBERRY DAIQUIRI

Serves 4

"This drink has a touch of banana and can be made about 2 hours before serving if kept in freezer."

1 (6-ounce) can frozen limeade
 concentrate
1 (10-ounce) pkg. frozen
 strawberries
½ C. rum
½ C. Maker's Mark
1 ripe banana
6 ice cubes, or more as needed

- Blend all ingredients with ice in electric blender.
- Serve immediately or store in freezer for short periods of time while serving.

THE MAKER'S SLUSH

"A beverage you will want to keep in the freezer for impulsive entertaining."

2 (3-ounce) boxes strawberry
    gelatin
3 C. hot water
3 C. sugar (less is better)
3 C. cold water
2 small cans frozen lemonade
2 large cans unsweetened
    pineapple juice
1 large can unsweetened
    orange juice
1 C. Maker's Mark
2 (10-ounce) pkgs. frozen
    strawberries or 1 qt. fresh

- Combine gelatin and boiling water till thoroughly dissolved, then add sugar, mixing well.
- Add cold water, juices, and bourbon. Stir in strawberries. Freeze this mixture in plastic containers.
- About three hours before serving time, remove from freezer to semi-thaw.
- When ready to serve, put in punch bowl; add frozen or fresh strawberries and stir until slushy.

BOURBON-ORANGE COOLER

"An easy drink that will delight any guest."

1¼ ounces Maker's Mark
3 ounces champagne
3 ounces orange juice

- Add ingredients to tall drink glass filled with ice; stir.
- Garnish with fresh orange wedge.

SPARKLING PUNCH

"Always add carbonated beverages to punch just before serving to prevent from going flat."

2 (10-ounces each) pkgs. frozen
    strawberries, thawed
1½ C. Maker's Mark
1 C. lemon juice
¾ C. water
1 (6-ounce) can frozen orange
    juice concentrate, thawed
Ice cubes (can be made of
    frozen orange juice)
2 (28-ounces each) bottles
    ginger ale, chilled.

- Mix strawberries, bourbon, lemon juice, water and orange juice concentrate; refrigerate until cold, at least 2 hours.
- Pour fruit mixture over ice cubes in punch bowl; stir in ginger ale.
- Garnish punch with mint sprigs if desired.

"Bill Samuels believes three things can go wrong in making a perfect mint julep. The first is using a low-grade bourbon that has a strong, hot bite. The next mistake is using too much mint to cover up the bourbon's strong bite. The last is an over-infusion of sugar to cover up the mint. Try this special mint julep."

*1 bottle of Maker's Mark
    (90 proof bourbon whisky)*
Fresh mint
Water, preferably distilled
Granulated sugar
*Garnish with mint sprigs and
    powdered sugar (optional)*

- To prepare *mint extract,* pick mint and remove leaves smaller than a dime. Wash, pat dry put 40 leaves in mixing bowl and cover with 3 ounces of Maker's Mark.

- Allow leaves to soak in bourbon for 15 minutes.

- Gather leaves in bundle, put in clean cotton cloth and wring vigorously over bowl where leaves soaked– bruising leaves. Keep dipping in bourbon (several times) and wringing leaves so juice of mint is dripped back into bourbon. Let this mint extract set.

- For *simple syrup,* mix equal amounts of granulated sugar and water into cooking pot. (ex. 1 cup sugar and 1 cup water.) Heat long enough for sugar to dissolve in water. Stir so sugar doesn't burn. Remove from heat and let cool. This can be done several hours in advance.

- For *julep mixture,* pour 3½ parts of Maker's Mark to 1 part simple syrup into large bowl. Begin adding mint extract in small portions. You must taste and smell– there is no formula since each extract will vary in strength. Pour finished julep stock in covered jar and refrigerate at least 24 hours to "marry" the flavors.

- To serve julep, fill each silver julep cup ½ full with shaved ice; insert a mint sprig.

- Pack in more ice to about 1 inch over top of each cup. Insert straw that has been cut to no more than one inch from above top of cup so nose is forced to sniff the "bloom" when sipping julep.

- When frost forms on glass, pour refrigerated julep mixture over ice and sprinkle powdered sugar on top if desired.

- You have made a perfect mint julep the Bill Samuels' way.

BEEF TIDBITS WITH HORSERADISH SAUCE — *Serves 30–40*

"This dish also makes a tasty entrée for any meal."

1 (4-lb.) eye-of-round roast

MARINADE
1 C. soy sauce
¼ C. Maker's Mark
½ C. oil
3 cloves garlic, crushed

HORSERADISH SAUCE
1 C. heavy cream
1 C. mayonnaise
Pinch of salt
¼ C. horseradish or to taste

- Combine marinade ingredients and pour over roast which has been placed in pyrex dish. Cover with plastic wrap and marinate in refrigerator 24-48 hours, turning 3–4 times.
- Remove meat from marinade; towel dry and roast at 350° for about 1 hour. Use meat thermometer and cook to medium-rare.
- Cool immediately in refrigerator; slice very thin for small sandwiches.
- Serve with Parker House rolls and horseradish sauce.
- Whip cream until soft peaks form; beat in mayonnaise and salt until well mixed. Thoroughly blend in horseradish with spoon.
- Serve with roast beef sandwiches. For lighter sauce, omit the mayonnaise.

WHISKY SOUR PUNCH — *Serves 20*

*"An alternative to preparing individual drinks.
Let everyone dip the punch."*

4 C. Maker's Mark
4 (6-ounce) cans frozen
   lemonade, thawed
2 qts. apple juice or cider
2 qts. ginger ale
1 (10-ounce) bottle
   maraschino cherries
Block of ice to fit punch bowl.

- Combine all ingredients.
- Serve immediately in punch bowl that has a block of ice in it. Be sure to hollow out a shallow cavity in top of ice block for cherries and surround entire block with punch.
- *Hint*—Ice block can be frozen in waxed ½ gallon milk carton.

PARTY STYLE – CLASSIC PUNCH — *Serves 20*

"A delicious and pretty punch that bubbles!"

2 qts. pineapple juice, chilled
2 qts. cranberry juice, chilled
1 (12-ounce) can frozen orange
   juice concentrate, thawed
2 C. Maker's Mark, chilled
2 qts. 7-Up, chilled
3 magnums champagne,
   chilled
Pineapple or rainbow sherbet

- Combine juices in a punch bowl.
- When ready to serve, stir in bourbon, 7-Up and champagne.
- Float scoops of sherbet in punch.

MAKER'S FRANKS

*"This appetizer may be prepared a day in advance,
refrigerated and reheated."*

½ C. chopped onion
½ C. chopped green pepper
¼ C. butter
4 (8-ounce) cans tomato sauce
1 C. plus 2 Tbs. brown sugar
1 (12-ounce) can tomato paste
1 C. Maker's Mark
4 tsp. Worcestershire sauce
4 tsp. wine vinegar
4 tsp. prepared mustard
1 tsp. minced garlic
¼–½ tsp. salt
¼ tsp. pepper
4–5 drops Tabasco sauce
3–4 lbs. frankfurters, cut in
   1-inch pieces

- Sauté onion and green pepper in butter until soft and add remaining ingredients–except frankfurters. Bring to a boil, then reduce heat.
- Add frankfurters and simmer for 1 hour. Transfer to heated chafing dish and provide wooden picks.
- These frankfurters, simmered in a bourbon sauce, are delicious. The alcohol evaporates in the cooking process, but it lends a distinctive flavor to the sauce.

SURPRISE PECANS

"An unusual blend of flavors."

3 ounces crumbled Roquefort
   cheese
1 (3-ounce) pkg. cream cheese
120 pecan halves
2 tsp. Maker's Mark

- Mix cheeses that are at room temperature with bourbon.
- Spread mixture on flat side of pecan halves and press together, sandwich fashion.
- Refrigerate, but remove about 2 hours before serving— always serve cheese at room temperature.

SPIKED CRANBERRY COCKTAIL

"Beautiful served in a silver punch bowl."

1 qt. cranberry juice
1 (10½-ounce) can pineapple
   juice
1 C. orange juice
½ C. lemon juice
1½ C. Maker's Mark
1 (48-ounce) bottle ginger ale
   or more

- Mix juices and refrigerate overnight.
- When ready to serve, add chilled bourbon and ginger ale.
- Assorted fruits such as strawberries, pineapple and lemons can be added to punch.

MAKER'S MARK EGGNOG
Yields 2½ gallons

"A Christmas tradition."

2 doz. eggs
1½ C. sugar
1 liter Maker's Mark
1 qt. heavy cream
1 qt. milk
Nutmeg as garnish

- Separate eggs and beat yolks until creamy. Whip all sugar into yolks.
- Beat whites until they stand in peaks, adding ½ cup of extra sugar, if desired.
- Beat yolks and whisky together, stirring whisky in slowly with wire whisk to prevent curdling.
- Blend cream and add milk last. Add nutmeg to taste and garnish top of each serving with nutmeg.
- *Hint:* Should be made several hours before serving or refrigerated overnight. Need large bowls for mixing and storing in refrigerator.

CHUTNEY DIP
Yields 2 cups

"So easy for quick party fare."

16 ounces cream cheese, softened
1 tsp. seasoned salt
½ tsp. curry powder
⅓ C. chutney, chopped if in large chunks
½–1 C. sour cream
3 Tbs. Maker's Mark

- Beat cream cheese with mixer until smooth; add remaining ingredients.
- Chill until ready to use.
- Serve as dip for fresh fruit.

CHEESE RING
Serves 16

"Really different and looks pretty on the table."

16 ounces sharp cheddar cheese, grated
1 C. pecans, chopped
¾ C. mayonnaise
1 medium onion, grated
1 clove garlic, pressed
2 Tbs. Maker's Mark
1 C. strawberry preserves or cranberry chutney

- Combine all ingredients except preserves and mix well.
- Mold into ring and chill.
- When ready to serve, fill with preserves or chutney and serve with crackers.

PEACH BOURBONED MEATBALLS

"Serve this superb appetizer at your fanciest party."

2 lbs. ground round
¾ C. milk
½ C. bread crumbs
1 Tbs. Worcestershire sauce
1½ tsp. salt
1 tsp. garlic powder
¼ tsp. nutmeg
¼ tsp. ground ginger
⅛ tsp. ground pepper
2 drops hot pepper sauce
2 Tbs. melted shortening or oil
Bourbon Peach Sauce
  (see below)
1 Tbs. cornstarch (if needed)
1 Tbs. cold water (if needed)

BOURBON PEACH SAUCE

1 (1-lb., 2-ounce) jar peach
  preserves
¾ C. packed brown sugar
½ C. Maker's Mark
½ C. marmalade (peach
  or orange)
¼ tsp. nutmeg

- Blend first 10 ingredients together in bowl. Shape mixture into 1½–2 inch balls.
- In large skillet or electric fry pan, brown meatballs in hot shortening. Remove with slotted spoon, set aside and keep warm.
- Combine Bourbon Peach Sauce ingredients in bowl. Lower heat, blend sauce mixture into meat drippings and simmer for 10 minutes.
- Add meatballs to sauce and coat thoroughly. Cover and simmer for 45 minutes to 1 hour. If necessary, blend cornstarch with cold water to form paste, add to sauce, stirring constantly, and cook over low heat until thickened.
- Transfer to chafing dish for buffet service.

BOURBON BOLO

"Not only delicious, but beautiful when served over ice block!"

1 diced fresh pineapple
1 C. simple syrup
1 (750ml) Maker's Mark
2 (750ml) champagne
Ice block

- Mix pineapple, simple syrup and bourbon. Let set for 12 hours.
- When ready to serve, place decorative block of ice or whole fresh frozen pineapple in punch bowl.
- Pour pineapple mixture over it and add champagne.
- To make ice block, fill ½ gallon waxed milk carton with distilled water and freeze. If flowers are desired in ice block, fill ¼ full of water; after it is frozen, add greenery or flowers and fill to ½. Freeze again, add more flowers and fill to top.
- Remember to add champagne just before serving.

"Lovely centerpiece for any party."

2 cups fresh pineapple
1 qt. fresh strawberries
¾ lb. powdered sugar
1 C. Maker's Mark
2 C. lemon juice
1½ C. orange juice
1 C. grenadine
2 (750ml) bottles of
  Maker's Mark
2 qts. chilled carbonated water
  or ginger ale
1-50 lb. cube of ice

- Slice pineapple, place in large bowl and crush; add strawberries and sprinkle sugar over fruit; pour bourbon over fruit, allowing to stand, covered, for 4 hours.

- To above mixture, add next 4 ingredients; place mixture in ice punch bowl, stirring to blend and chill.

- Just before serving, add carbonated water or ginger ale.

- For serving, choose a large round metal bowl—at least 3-quart capacity. Chip out a small depression in center of ice block and set bowl over it.

- Fill bowl with boiling water being careful not to spill any on ice beneath. Stir water, as heat from the bowl melts ice. As water cools, empty and refill bowl until hole in ice is large enough for bowl to set in.

- Move completed block of ice to a tray of foil where you're serving punch. Tray should be 2 inches larger than ice and turned up in gutter fashion to catch melting water; fill ice bowl with punch.

- Lay flowers around foil to hide it; this idea could also be used for serving sherbets or mixing cocktails.

- *Hint*—this ice block sounds difficult, but it's not—a great conversation piece.

"If you're in a hurry, ⅓ cup teriyaki sauce can be substituted for the marinade mixture."

1 Tbs. minced onion
1 clove garlic, minced
1 tsp. Worcestershire sauce
¼ C. soy sauce
1 Tbs. sugar
¼ tsp. ground ginger
¼ tsp. salt
½ lb. round steak or sirloin,
  cut diagonally into very
  thin strips
1 (6-ounce) can water
  chestnuts, halved
1 C. Maker's Mark Gourmet
  Sauce

- Combine onion, garlic, Worcestershire sauce, soy sauce, sugar, ginger and salt. Coat meat strips evenly in this mixture and marinate for 30 minutes, stirring occasionally.

- Drain strips and wrap around water chestnuts, securing with a toothpick.

- Arrange in a shallow glass baking dish and cook in microwave for 3–4 minutes on full power. Rest 5 minutes after cooking.

- Serve hot with Gourmet Sauce for dipping.

THE MAKER'S PERCOLATOR PUNCH

*"Serve from percolator—letting each guest fill cup when needed—
and what a delightful fragrance."*

2 (32-ounce each) bottles
　cranberry juice cocktail

1 (46-ounce) can pineapple
　juice

2 C. water

1 C. packed brown sugar

¼ tsp. salt

4 tsp. whole cloves

4 sticks cinnamon, broken
　in pieces

Peel of ¼ orange, cut in strips

1½ C. Maker's Mark

- In a 24-cup automatic percolator, combine cranberry juice, pineapple juice, water, brown sugar and salt.

- Place cloves, cinnamon pieces and orange peel in coffee maker basket. Assemble coffee maker; plug in and percolate.

- Just before serving, remove basket and add Maker's Mark.

WASSAIL PUNCH

*"An English Christmas drink that means 'be in health'. It was the
custom in England years ago to toast the lord of the manor with this
traditional punch."*

1 gallon apple cider

1 (12-ounce) can frozen
　orange juice concentrate

1½ C. water

1 (6-ounce) can lemonade
　concentrate

16 whole cloves

4 cinnamon sticks, broken into
　pieces

1 tsp. each of nutmeg, ground
　cinnamon and ground cloves

2 C. Maker's Mark

1 orange, sliced

1 lemon, sliced

- In large pot combine all ingredients, except orange and lemon slices; heat mixture to boiling, then reduce to simmer. Simmer for 10 minutes to blend flavors.

- To serve, float orange or lemon slices on top—can be served hot or cold.

ZUCCHINI SOUP WITH ZEST

*"This soup is wonderful for using all those surplus zucchini—
everyone will think you're a genius!"*

3 Tbs. butter
2–3 medium red onions,
 thinly sliced
1 large clove garlic, minced
1 tsp. curry powder
6 large zucchini, sliced
 ¼-inch thick
2–3 tsp. salt
Freshly ground pepper
3 C. chicken stock
Lemon juice
Cayenne pepper
1½ C. heavy cream
1½ Tbs. Maker's Mark

- In large saucepan, sauté onions and garlic in butter until soft. Stir in curry powder and cook slowly, about 2 minutes.
- Add zucchini, cover and cook over low heat for 6 minutes.
- Add chicken stock, cover and simmer about 8 minutes or until zucchini is tender, but crisp.
- Puree in blender. Do not let this puree become too smooth.
- Season to taste with salt, pepper, lemon juice and a few dashes of cayenne pepper.
- Stir in cream and bourbon immediately before serving.

AFTERNOON STEW

"A great stew for coming home to after a long day."

2 lbs. beef stew meat
1 can mushrooms
¾ C. water
¼ C. Maker's Mark
1 can mushroom soup
1 env. dry onion soup mix

- Preheat oven to 325°.
- Mix all ingredients in casserole; cover.
- Bake in 325° oven for 3 hours.
- Serve with freshly baked biscuits.

CLASSIC ONION SOUP

*"Red onions make the difference in this soup. In fact, one of my special
secrets is to always buy red onions for cooking."*

5 C. thinly sliced red onions
3 Tbs. butter
3 Tbs. flour
½ C. Maker's Mark
2 qts. beef bouillon or broth
¼ tsp. basil or to taste
1 slice toasted French or Italian
 bread, per person
½ C. grated Swiss cheese

- In a dutch oven (or heavy pan), sauté sliced onions in butter until soft.
- Stir in flour to form a paste; pour in bourbon, stirring until smooth.
- Gradually stir in bouillon; season with basil and simmer 30–40 minutes.
- Drop into bottom of each soup bowl a slice of toasted Italian bread, fill with onion soup and sprinkle with cheese. Broil until cheese is golden and bubbly.
- Serve immediately.

COLD FRUIT SOUP

Serves 6

"A summer delight served as an appetizer, main course or dessert."

½ C. dried apricots
¼ C. dark raisins
¼ C. golden raisins
½ C. diced fresh peaches
1½ C. water
¼ C. Maker's Mark
1 cinnamon stick
4 C. apple cider
2 C. of mixed chopped fresh
  fruit, such as plums,
  strawberries, apricots,
  blueberries, nectarines
  and/or mangos

- Place dried fruits in a deep saucepan; add water, bourbon and cinnamon stick. Simmer over medium heat for about 30 minutes or until dried fruits are soft. Remove cinnamon stick.
- Pour fruit mixture into blender and puree until smooth.
- Pour puree back into saucepan. Return cinnamon stick, add apple cider and simmer until hot.
- Add mixed fresh fruits and cook for 5–10 minutes or until all fruits are very soft. Remove cinnamon stick.
- Chill for 2 hours in refrigerator and serve cold.

CHRISTMAS SOUP

Serves 4

*"Serve this deep-rose colored soup, topped with sour cream
and parsley for the holidays."*

2 C. diced uncooked beets
½ onion, sliced
1 chicken bouillon cube
3 C. water
4 ounces cream cheese,
  softened
2 Tbs. Maker's Mark
Salt and pepper to taste

- In saucepan, combine the beets, onion, bouillon cube and water. Cook, covered, until the beets are soft.
- Pour into a blender, cover and whirl until the beets are finely chopped. Add the cream cheese and bourbon, cover and blend thoroughly. Salt and pepper to taste.
- This soup can be served either hot or cold.

AUTUMN SOUP

Serves 6

"This cream soup is perfect for a ladies' luncheon, such a rich color."

6 Tbs. butter or margarine
2 leeks, chopped, white
  part only
2 stalks celery, chopped
1 onion, chopped
3 C. pumpkin puree
6 C. chicken bouillon
1 C. heavy cream
Salt to taste
Freshly ground pepper
  to taste
¼ C. Maker's Mark

- Sauté leeks, celery and onion in butter until limp, about 8 minutes. Stir in pumpkin puree.
- Add chicken bouillon. Cover pan and simmer for 30 minutes.
- Stir in cream and season with salt and pepper.
- Add bourbon and bring to a boil.
- Serve immediately.

CLAM AND KENTUCKY VEGETABLE CHOWDER   *Yields 10 cups*

"A hearty soup served with bread and salad."

3 C. water

3 chicken-flavored
  bouillon cubes

4 medium potatoes, peeled
  and diced

1 medium onion, sliced

1 C. thinly sliced carrot

½ C. diced green pepper

⅓ C. butter

⅓ C. all-purpose flour

3½ C. milk

3 C. (¾ lb.) shredded sharp
  Cheddar cheese

1 (2-ounce) jar diced
  pimento, drained

3 Tbs. Maker's Mark

2 (6½-ounce each) cans
  minced clams

¼ tsp. hot sauce (optional)

Fresh parsley

- Combine water and bouillon cubes in a Dutch oven; bring to a boil. Add vegetables; cover and simmer 12 minutes or until vegetables are tender.
- Melt butter in a heavy saucepan over low heat; add flour, stirring until smooth. Cook 1 minute, stirring constantly.
- Gradually add milk; cook over medium heat, stirring constantly until thickened and bubbly. Add cheese, stirring until melted.
- Stir cheese sauce, pimento, bourbon, clams and hot sauce into vegetable mixture. Cook over low heat until thoroughly heated (do not boil).
- Garnish with a parsley sprig and serve.

KENTUCKY BEEF STEW   *Serves 6*

"Serve this thick soup with crusty French bread."

3 lbs. beef chuck, cut into
  1½-inch cubes

Salt and freshly ground
  black pepper

6 Tbs. (¾ stick) butter

12–15 small boiling onions,
  peeled

⅔ C. very strong beef stock or
  undiluted condensed
  beef broth

½ C. Maker's Mark

1 large garlic clove (pressed)

6 carrots, peeled and cut into
  2-inch strips

4 tsp. grated fresh lemon peel

4 Tbs. finely chopped fresh
  parsley

- Season meat generously with salt and pepper.
- Heat butter in large heavy kettle or Dutch oven over medium heat until it bubbles and begins to brown.
- Add meat, turning each piece to coat with butter; arrange onions over meat.
- Stir together stock, only ¼ cup bourbon now, and garlic; add to meat. Cover and cook without stirring over very low heat about 2½ hours or until meat is tender.
- Stir and add carrots. Cover and simmer just until tender, about 30 minutes.
- Gently stir in lemon peel, remaining ¼ cup bourbon and only 2 tablespoons parsley. Taste and add more salt, if necessary.
- Ladle into shallow soup plates. Sprinkle with remaining parsley.

SEAFOOD BISQUE

Serves 6

"This soup can be made with minced shrimp instead of crab."

1 pt. milk
2 pieces lemon peel
½ tsp. mace (ground)
1 lb. white crabmeat
½ stick butter
1 pt. light cream
¼ C. cracker crumbs
Salt and pepper to taste
2 Tbs. Maker's Mark

- Put milk into top of double boiler and simmer with lemon peel for a few minutes.
- Add crab, butter, cream and mace; cook for 15 minutes.
- Thicken with cracker crumbs; season with salt and pepper and allow to stand on back of stove for a few minutes to bring out flavor.
- Just before serving, add bourbon.

CHILLED CANTALOUPE SOUP

Serves 6

"Serve in cut glass bowls for an impressive dish."

1 ripe cantaloupe, peeled,
   seeded and cut into chunks
¼ C. Maker's Mark
2 Tbs. honey
1 Tbs. fresh lime juice
Fresh mint

- Put all ingredients into food processor or blender and mix well.
- Cover and chill in refrigerator.
- Blend again before serving and serve garnished with mint leaves.

STRAWBERRY SOUP

Yields 3½ cups

"Soup is especially delicious and colorful served in cantaloupe shells which have been halved and seeded — what creative soup bowls for a luncheon."

2 C. strawberries, sliced
1 C. sour cream
1 C. half-and-half
¼ C. sugar
1½ Tbs. Maker's Mark
1 tsp. vanilla extract
Whole strawberries,
   for garnish

- Combine all ingredients, except extra strawberries for garnishing, in electric blender; process until smooth.
- Pour into chilled soup bowls or cantaloupe shells. Garnish each serving with whole strawberries.

WILTED SPINACH SALAD
Serves 4

"This bourbon dressing is also special served over early spring lettuce and onions from your garden."

1 lb. fresh spinach, cleaned
  and stems removed
1 Tbs. shallots
2 strips bacon (uncooked)
1 tsp. butter
2 ounces red wine vinegar
4 mushrooms, thinly sliced
2 Tbs. Maker's Mark
4 ounces crumbled Bleu
  Cheese

- Clean and rinse spinach thoroughly.
- In a small pan, lightly sauté shallots and bacon in butter; drain bacon, break into pieces and return to pan.
- Add red wine vinegar and mushrooms.
- Flame mixture with bourbon.
- In large bowl, toss spinach and bleu cheese with hot vinegar/bourbon mixture until all leaves are thoroughly coated.
- Serve immediately.

CANTALOUPE—THE HIGHLANDS WAY
Serves 8

"Melon can be filled with grapes only—if you prefer—an excellent salad or dessert."

1 large cantaloupe
Maker's Mark (enough to
  fill melon)

- Cut a hole 2″ in diameter in end of cantaloupe. Remove plug and with a long spoon, scoop out seeds.
- Fill cavity with variety of fresh fruits in season.
- Pour in enough bourbon to fill melon, replace plug and seal.
- Allow to age at least 4 hours.
- Slice melon in wedges and serve by mounding fruit and liquid on top of each slice.

HOT FRUIT SALAD
Serves 12

"Perfect when served on a cold rainy night."

Medium can sliced pineapple
Medium can peach halves
Medium can apple rings
Medium can pear halves
Medium can apricot halves

SAUCE
2 Tbs. flour
½ C. brown sugar
1 stick butter
¾ C. Maker's Mark
  (or adjust to taste)

- Drain fruit well and place in alternate layers in a 2-quart casserole dish.
- In top of double boiler, combine sauce ingredients. Cook, stirring over hot water, until thick and smooth.
- Pour hot sauce over fruit; cover and refrigerate overnight or several days. When ready to serve, heat in preheated 350° oven for 25–30 minutes until bubbly.

LEMON MOLD WITH BOURBON MAYONNAISE
Serves 8

*"A party salad—and for a festive mayonnaise, add a little beet juice
(from a can)—for a rich red color."*

2 (3-ounce) pkgs. lemon gelatin
½ C. shredded cabbage
½ C. shredded carrot
1 C. orange juice
½ C. diced green pepper
2 Tbs. chopped pimento
½ C. cauliflower bits (optional)

BOURBON MAYONNAISE
_____
1 C. mayonnaise
3 Tbs. Maker's Mark
½ Tbs. lemon juice

- Prepare gelatin according to package directions, using orange juice for one cup of cold water.
- Add vegetables; chill in large size ring mold.
- Serve on Bibb lettuce leaves or fill center of gelatin with chicken salad and garnish with tomato wedges.
- For mayonnaise, blend ingredients together and chill.
- Serve over Lemon Mold or vegetable salads. Also excellent spooned over tomato slices; delicious served as sauce for fish and cold meats.

ORANGE-PECAN SALAD DRESSING
Serves 8

"This easy dressing enhances any fruit salad."

1 (8-ounce) pkg. cream cheese, softened
1 (6-ounce) can concentrated orange juice, thawed (not diluted)
2 Tbs. Maker's Mark
1½ tsp. sugar
¼ tsp. salt
¼ C. chopped pecans

- Beat cream cheese until smooth.
- Add orange juice, bourbon, sugar and salt; beat until smooth. Stir in pecans.
- Refrigerate 8 hours or overnight to blend flavors.
- Remove from refrigerator an hour before serving to soften; mix with assorted cut fruits.

HOLIDAY SALAD DRESSING
Serves 6

"Have fruit ready in bowl—and just before serving, add dressing."

3 Tbs. orange juice
3 Tbs. lemon juice
4 Tbs. pineapple juice
2 Tbs. flour
2 eggs
⅓ C. sugar
½ C. cream, whipped
1 Tbs. Maker's Mark

- Heat fruit juices; mix sugar and flour together and slowly add the hot fruit juices.
- Cook in double boiler 15 minutes, stirring constantly.
- Pour slowly over well-beaten eggs and cook for 2 minutes more; cool.
- Just before serving, add whipped cream and bourbon; beat until fluffy.
- Serve over any fruit salad.

SCENIC CHICKEN SALAD

"Since no mayonnaise is used in the dressing, this is an ideal salad to pack into the picnic basket—no matter how hot the day—and great for a family reunion."

3 whole chicken breasts, poached
½ lb. thinly sliced boiled ham
½ lb. bean sprouts
½ C. walnuts
Salt and pepper
¾ C. olive oil
¼ C. soy sauce
2 Tbs. Maker's Mark
Lettuce

- Remove all skin and bones from chicken and use a sharp knife to cut meat into long julienne strips of matchstick thickness.
- Cut the boiled ham into strips of same size and combine two meats in a mixing bowl.
- Add bean sprouts and sprinkle lightly with salt and pepper.
- Prepare dressing by beating together oil, soy sauce, bourbon, nuts, salt and pepper.
- Pour dressing over salad and toss well.
- Serve on lettuce leaves with Lemon Mold (recipe in this section).

PEANUT BUTTER WALDORF SALAD

"Enjoy fruit the easy way."

1 C. plain yogurt
¼ C. sugar
¼ C. crunchy peanut butter
2 Tbs. Maker's Mark
4 medium red apples, chopped
½ C. chopped celery
½ C. raisins

- Combine yogurt, sugar and peanut butter in bowl; mix well and add bourbon.
- Add apples, celery and raisins; toss lightly.
- Chill until serving time.

BLACK CHERRY SALAD

"A salad served every Christmas Eve at our house—really delicious!"

1 (3-ounce) pkg. of black cherry gelatin
1 (no. 303) can of black cherries
1 C. of hot water
¾ C. of cherry juice
¼ C. plus 1 Tbs. Maker's Mark
Juice of 1 lemon
3 ounces cream cheese
¾ C. of broken pecans

- Dissolve gelatin in hot water; add cherry juice drained from canned, seedless cherries. Add ¼ cup of Maker's Mark and lemon juice.
- Add cherries and pour mixture into a mold and refrigerate—until slightly jelled.
- While cherry mixture is jelling, mix 1 tablespoon Maker's Mark with cream cheese, add pecans and form into small balls with melon ball utensil.
- Stir pecan balls into slightly jelled cherry mixture and return to refrigerate until firm.
- Serve on salad greens.

MIXED GREENS WITH BOURBON DRESSING

Yields 3½ cups

*"Excellent dressing for mixed greens, main course
vegetables or seafood salads."*

2 C. olive oil
1 C. vinegar
2 Tbs. Maker's Mark
4 Tbs. tomato catsup
½ tsp. salt
2 Tbs. sugar
½ tsp. sesame seed
6 whole cloves
3–4 dashes tabasco

- Mix all ingredients in a jar or bottle.
- Shake well and allow to stand for 48 hours—*not* in the refrigerator.
- Shake well before using.

TIPSY FRUIT

Serves 2

"An interesting way to serve fresh fruit."

2 Tbs. water
1 Tbs. sugar
1 Tbs. Maker's Mark
¼ tsp. powdered ginger
1 C. fresh pineapple chunks
1 C. fresh strawberries, sliced
Walnuts for garnish

- Combine first 4 ingredients in a small saucepan; simmer over low heat until sugar dissolves. Remove from heat and let cool.
- Combine sugar mixture and pineapple chunks; cover and chill at least 1 hour.
- Add strawberries; garnish with walnuts, cover and chill thoroughly.
- Serve fruit a few hours after preparation for best results.

SWEET POTATO CASSEROLE SURPRISE

Serves 10

"The best casserole ever."

6 medium-size sweet potatoes
  (about 4 lbs.)
½ C. butter or margarine,
  melted
½ C. firmly packed
  brown sugar
⅓ C. orange juice
¼ C. Maker's Mark
½ tsp. salt
½ tsp. pumpkin pie spice

TOPPING

1 C. brown sugar
½ C. flour
½ stick margarine
1 C. chopped nuts

- Cook sweet potatoes in boiling water for 20–25 minutes or until tender; drain and let cool to touch.
- Peel potatoes and mash pulp.
- Combine potatoes and next 6 ingredients, mixing well. Spoon mixture into a lightly greased 1½-quart baking dish.
- Mix together topping ingredients and cover sweet potato mixture.
- Bake at 375° for 40 minutes.

HAPPY CRANBERRIES

Yields 3 cups

"A fancy Southern side dish."

1 lb. fresh cranberries
2 C. sugar
4 Tbs. Maker's Mark
¼ C. sugar

- Place berries in a shallow pan. Sprinkle with 2 cups sugar.
- Bake covered at 350° for one hour.
- Remove from oven and sprinkle with bourbon and remaining sugar.
- Refrigerate—ready to serve anytime. Also makes a super gift—just fill a small jar for giving!

SAFFRON-BOURBON PILAF

Serves 6

"A new twist for rice lovers."

¼ C. butter
2 Tbs. olive oil
2 C. rice
1 small onion, minced
4 C. chicken broth
1/16 tsp. saffron
1–2 Tbs. Maker's Mark
⅓ C. slivered, toasted almonds

- Melt butter and olive oil in a large saucepan.
- Stir in rice and onion, cooking over low heat until rice is lightly colored.
- Add broth and saffron and bring to a boil. Reduce heat and cover tightly; cook 20–25 minutes or until liquid is absorbed.
- Sprinkle with toasted almonds and bourbon; fluff with a fork and serve.

SWEET POTATOES IN ORANGE CUPS

Serves 4

"I've been using this recipe for years."

2 oranges
4 sweet potatoes
4 tsp. butter or margarine
¼ tsp. salt
4 tsp. brown sugar
⅛ C. orange juice
2 Tbs. Maker's Mark
4 marshmallows

- Wash and dry oranges. Cut into halves, remove pulp and membrane and set skins aside to be used as shells.
- Scrub sweet potatoes; bake in 375° oven for 45 minutes or until tender.
- Cool, remove skins and mash.
- Add butter or margarine, salt, sugar, bourbon and orange juice, then beat sweet potatoes until light and fluffy.
- Fill orange shells with mashed sweet potato and place a marshmallow on each. Place in baking pan and bake in moderate oven (350°) for 15 minutes or until top is slightly glazed. Serve hot.

BAKED BEANS WITH MAKER'S

Serves 16

"Wonderful addition to a picnic basket or a party."

4 (1 lb.) cans baked beans
1 Tbs. molasses
½ C. strong coffee
¾ tsp. dry mustard
½ C. chili sauce
⅓ C. Maker's Mark
12 slices canned pineapple
Brown sugar

- Place all ingredients except pineapple and sugar in a large baking dish. Cover, let stand 3 hours at room temperature.
- Preheat oven to 375°; bake, covered, about 35 minutes.
- Uncover, arrange pineapple on beans, brush liberally with brown sugar and continue baking about 30 minutes.

BOURBONED SQUASH RINGS

Serves 8

"This dish is also exceptional when reheated the next day— if there's any left."

2 large acorn squash, cut into
    ½-inch rings and seeded
4 Tbs. Maker's Mark
¼ C. butter, melted
2 Tbs. brown sugar
¼ tsp. freshly grated nutmeg

- Preheat oven to 375°; line baking dish with aluminum foil.
- Arrange squash rings in single layer on foil. Prick with fork and brush rings generously with bourbon. Let stand 5 minutes to absorb liquor.
- Brush evenly with melted butter; sprinkle with brown sugar and nutmeg.
- Bake until tender, about 20 minutes.
- Serve immediately.

FLAMED MUSHROOMS

Serves 6

*"This dish can be served as a vegetable or poured over
steaks as a sauce."*

1 lb. fresh mushrooms
6 Tbs. butter
1 tsp. fresh lemon juice
¼ tsp. salt
½ tsp. pepper
3 Tbs. Maker's Mark
½ C. heavy cream, heated

- Wash mushrooms and trim stems.
- Melt butter, add lemon juice, salt and pepper; heat
  and add mushrooms. Sauté until browned.
- Drain mushrooms; pour bourbon over them
  and ignite.
- When flame dies, stir in heated heavy cream and
  serve immediately.

SAUCY CARROT SLICES

Serves 4

"What a way to get your vitamins."

2 (15-ounce) cans sliced
  carrots, drained
¼ C. orange marmalade
1 Tbs. soy sauce
1 tsp. lemon juice
1 Tbs. Maker's Mark (or more)

- In saucepan over medium-high heat, bring carrots,
  orange marmalade, soy sauce and lemon juice to boil,
  stirring frequently.
- Take off burner and stir in bourbon.
- Serve immediately.

ORANGE RICE

Serves 12

"Rice at its very best."

1 C. white raisins
3 Tbs. Maker's Mark
½ C. butter
1 C. diced celery and leaves
4 Tbs. onion
4 Tbs. grated orange peel
2 C. orange juice
2 C. water
1 tsp. salt
1 (19-ounce) box minute rice

- Soak raisins in bourbon for 1 hour.
- Melt butter, adding celery, onion, and orange peel; cook
  until tender.
- Add orange juice, water and salt, bring to a boil and
  turn off heat. Stir in rice, raisins and bourbon; let
  stand, covered, at least 5 minutes, or put in warm oven
  until ready to serve.

HARVEST BREAD

"You may want to add more bourbon and less orange juice."

3½ C. flour
½ tsp. salt
1 tsp. nutmeg
1 tsp. cinnamon
2 tsp. soda
1 C. cooking oil
4 eggs, well beaten
3 C. white sugar
⅓ C. orange juice
⅓ C. Maker's Mark
1 C. raisins or dates
½ C. chopped pecans or
    walnuts
2 C. pumpkin

- Grease and flour 4 (1-lb.) coffee cans.
- Sift together all dry ingredients; then add other ingredients in listed order. Mix thoroughly, pour into coffee cans, filling each about ½–⅓ full.
- Bake at 350° until done—about 1 hour.
- Serve hot or cold.

EGGNOG FRUIT BREAD

"Give one away, keep one—you deserve it."

2¼ C. all-purpose flour
2 tsp. baking powder
¾ C. sugar
1 tsp. salt
1 C. chopped mixed
    candied fruit
½ C. chopped pecans
2 eggs, beaten
1 C. eggnog
¼ C. melted butter
½ C. confectioners' sugar
3 Tbs. Maker's Mark

- Preheat oven to 350°.
- Combine flour, baking powder, sugar and salt in bowl. Mix in fruit and pecans.
- Add mixture of eggs, eggnog and butter; mix just until moistened.
- Spoon into greased 5x9-inch loaf pan and bake for 1 hour and 10 minutes or until loaf tests done.
- Remove to wire rack to cool.
- Combine confectioners' sugar and bourbon in bowl; mix until smooth. Spoon over loaf.

CRANBERRY NUT BREAD
Serves 12

*"Remember to keep cranberries in your freezer all year long—
they are delicious at any season."*

1 C. raisins
⅓ C. Maker's Mark
½ C. butter
½ C. brown sugar, light
6 Tbs. orange marmalade
¾ C. small-curd creamed
    cottage cheese
2 eggs
Grated rind of 1 orange
¼ C. orange juice
3¾ C. flour
1 Tbs. baking powder
1 tsp. baking soda
½ tsp. salt
½ tsp. cinnamon
¼ tsp. each of ginger and
    allspice
1 C. cranberries, coarsely
    chopped
1 C. coarsely chopped nuts

- Chop frozen cranberries in a food processor (when frozen they are not so messy).
- Combine raisins and bourbon and set aside.
- Cream butter and sugar until light and fluffy; stir in marmalade.
- Beat in cottage cheese, eggs, orange rind and juice.
- Measure flour and sift with remaining dry ingredients. Stir the flour into cottage cheese mixture.
- Fold in raisins, bourbon, cranberries and nuts.
- Spoon into a well-greased 5x9-inch loaf pan and bake at 350° for 1½ hours.
- Cool in pan 10 minutes before removing to rack for cooling. (This bread also may be baked in two 3x7-inch loaf pans for about an hour.)

CHEESE BISCUITS
Yields 24

"This is a raised biscuit, delicious served with a salad meal."

2 C. flour
4 tsp. baking powder
1 tsp. salt
4 Tbs. shortening
1 C. grated cheese
⅔ C. milk (or more)

- Sift dry ingredients; add shortening and cheese. Mix into a wet dough with milk.
- Place on floured board and work only enough to handle well.
- Cut biscuits and bake in 425° oven for 10–12 minutes or until golden brown.
- Serve with Bourbon Butter (recipe in this section.)

BOURBON ROLLS

"These rolls are good enough for dessert."

⅓ C. cool water
1 pkg. yeast
2 Tbs. flour
2 C. scalded milk
2 eggs
½ – ⅔ C. shortening
   melted and cooled
½ C. sugar
2 tsp. salt
4 C. flour
Currants
1 added C. flour

ICING
1 Tbs. melted butter
1 C. powdered sugar
2 Tbs. Maker's Mark

- Beat the water, yeast and 2 tablespoons flour together. Let rise about 1 hour in warm place.
- Mix this with next six ingredients; beat thoroughly.
- Work in another cup of flour, mix to a smooth, but not-too-stiff dough.
- Refrigerate for 24 hours. (It will keep a week).
- Take small pieces of dough, walnut size, roll in the currants and put into small greased muffin pans. Let rise about 2 hours, until light.
- Bake in 375° oven for 15–20 minutes. (Use 2 well-greased muffin pans.)
- Frost generously with icing.
- For icing, mix together butter and sugar, thinning with about 2 tablespoons Maker's Mark.

BRUNCH CAKE

"A super coffee cake—very moist—and it actually gets better after second day."

1 (2-layer) yellow cake mix
4 eggs
½ C. oil
1 small pkg. instant vanilla
   pudding
6 ounces plain yogurt
6 ounces sour cream
3 Tbs. Maker's Mark
½ C. nuts (walnuts or pecans)

TOPPING
¾ C. brown sugar
1½ tsp. cinnamon

- Mix cake ingredients together in order given by beating with electric mixer.
- Pour ½ of cake mixture into greased bundt pan.
- Sprinkle with ½ of topping mixture.
- Put in rest of cake mixture; follow with rest of sugar mixture on top.
- Cut through with knife to swirl mixture.
- Bake in 325° oven for 55 minutes.

BOURBON PECAN BREAD

Yields 2 loaves

"This bread is similar to pound cake and is delicious toasted."

¾ C. raisins
⅓ C. Maker's Mark
1¼ sticks butter, softened
1½ C. sugar
6 eggs, separated
2¼ C. flour
1¼ tsp. vanilla
1 C. coarsely broken pecans

- Soak raisins in bourbon for 2 hours. Drain, reserving bourbon; if necessary, add more bourbon to make ⅓ cup.
- Generously grease two 5x9-inch (or smaller) loaf pans and line pan bottoms with greased wax paper; preheat oven to 350°.
- In a bowl, cream butter and ½ cup sugar until fluffy.
- Add egg yolks, one at a time, beating well; add flour in thirds, alternating with bourbon, mixing until well-blended.
- Stir in raisins, vanilla and pecans.
- In a large bowl, with clean beaters, beat egg whites until soft peaks form.
- Gradually beat in remaining 1 cup sugar, beating until stiff.
- Gently fold egg whites into batter.
- Turn batter into prepared loaf pans and bake for 1 hour or until done.

FRUITCAKE MUFFINS

Serves 30

"Muffins in a basket — absolutely wonderful holiday gift."

1 C. firmly packed brown
  sugar
¼ C. margarine
1½ C. flour
2 eggs, well beaten
1½ tsp. soda
1½ Tbs. milk
1 tsp. each cinnamon, allspice
1 lb. dates, chopped
½ lb. pecans, chopped
½ lb. candied cherries,
  chopped
½ lb. candied pineapple,
  chopped
1½ C. Maker's Mark

- Combine first 6 ingredients with spices in large bowl.
- Add dates, pecans, cherries and pineapple, reserving small amount for garnish. Sprinkle with bourbon; stir well.
- Line muffin tins with paper baking cups and fill muffin cups ⅔ full. Arrange reserved fruit and pecans on tops.
- Bake at 350° for about 20 minutes.

APRICOT CHRISTMAS BREAD

Yields 4 small loaves

*"This bread will remain fresh in refrigerator for several weeks—
great for gift giving!"*

1 (11-ounce) box apricots, diced
⅔ C. sugar
¼ C. Maker's Mark
¼ C. hot water
2 C. sugar
1 C. pecans, chopped
4 Tbs. butter
2 eggs
1 C. orange juice
4 C. plain flour
4 tsp. baking powder
½ tsp. soda
2 tsp. salt

- Soak diced apricots, sugar, bourbon and hot water overnight. Drain juice from apricots and SAVE. (This should be approximately ½ cup).

- Prepare 4 small loaf pans, grease, line with wax paper, then grease the wax paper. Preheat oven to 350°.

- Cream butter and sugar; add eggs one at a time, add orange juice and sifted, dry ingredients alternately.

- Then slowly add ½ cup reserved apricot liquid (drained from apricots); mix well.

- Add apricots and nuts, mixing well.

- Fill pans equally; let set for 10 minutes.

- Bake in preheated oven at 350° for 50–55 minutes or until a toothpick inserted in the middle of loaf comes out clean.

- When cool, wrap in foil or plastic wrap and refrigerate or freeze. *(Loaves store very well and remain fresh for weeks in the refrigerator.)*

- Serve with Bourbon Butter or spirited cream cheese.

BOURBON FRUIT BUTTER

Yields 4 cups

"A treat on pancakes, waffles or muffins."

1 (10-ounce) pkg. frozen
   raspberries or strawberries
¼ C. Maker's Mark
1 C. butter
2 C. powdered sugar

- Fruit and butter should be at room temperature.

- Cream butter and sugar; add berries and bourbon. Keep refrigerated.

"Bread may be frozen and is a real treat served with Bourbon Butter."

5½–6½ C. flour
2 Tbs. sugar
¼ C. soft shortening
2 pkgs. dry yeast
1 Tbs. salt
2½ C. very hot tap water

- Preheat oven to 400°.

- Mix dry yeast with 2 cups flour, sugar and salt in large bowl.

- Add shortening, then very hot water; beat two minutes at medium speed. Add 1 cup flour, beat 2 or more minutes.

- Stir in remaining flour gradually making a soft dough which leaves the sides of the bowl. Turn out onto floured board; knead 5-10 minutes.

- Cover with plastic wrap, then a cloth and let rest 20 minutes.

- Divide dough into two equal parts. Roll out to 8x12-inch size; shape into loaves by rolling (jelly roll style) and pressing together firmly. Seal securely and fold ends under, placing seam side down in well-greased loaf pan.

- Brush lightly with oil. Cover with wax paper, then plastic wrap.

- Refrigerate from 2–24 hours. Remove from refrigerator, uncover, let stand 10 minutes, carefully puncture any large bubbles.

- Bake in greased 5x9-inch loaf pans in 400° oven for 30–40 minutes.

- Remove from pans immediately. Brush with margarine and cool on racks.

BOURBON BUTTER

1 C. (2 sticks) unsalted butter, at
    room temperature
⅔ C. confectioners' sugar
¼ C. Maker's Mark

- Place the butter in a bowl and beat in the sugar and bourbon.

- For serving, place prepared mixture in ramekin and garnish with fresh mint or a strawberry.

OVERNIGHT WAFFLES WITH WHISKY CREME

Serves 6

"These waffles, made in crepe style, make a divine dessert."

2 C. milk
1 pkg. dry yeast
½ C. warm water
⅓ C. melted butter
1 tsp. salt
1 Tbs. sugar
3 C. flour
2 eggs, beaten
½ tsp. baking soda

WHISKY CREME

½ pt. whipped cream
1 Tbs. Maker's Mark
1 Tbs. powdered sugar
½ C. walnuts

- Scald milk; cool.
- Put water into large bowl, sprinkle in yeast, stir until dissolved.
- Add milk, butter, salt, sugar and flour; mix thoroughly with rotary beater until smooth. Cover and let stand at room temperature overnight.
- When ready to bake, add eggs and baking soda; beat well.
- Cook in well-greased, hot waffle iron until lightly browned.
- Serve with Whisky Creme or Bourbon Butter.
- To make Whisky Creme, fold bourbon into whipped cream; gently add sugar and walnuts and serve over waffles.

WHIPPED ORANGE BUTTER

Yields ¾ cup

*"Keep in refrigerator for emergency entertaining—
great served over cooked vegetables."*

½ C. butter, softened
2 Tbs. orange juice concentrate
2 Tbs. powdered sugar
1½ Tbs. finely grated
  orange rind

- Combine all ingredients in a food processor; process until smooth.
- Remove butter mixture to a small serving bowl and chill until ready to serve.

"NEVER FAIL" ROAST WITH PECAN SAUCE   *Serves any number*

"This recipe cooks any size roast brown on the outside and pink on the inside. Beef, lemon, pecans and mint – truly a winning combination."

Eye of round roast (or any roast size, but allow ½ – ¾ lb. per person)
Kitchen Bouquet
Salt and pepper to taste
1 stick butter

- Preheat oven to 500°.
- Put roast in pan and coat with Kitchen Bouquet; sprinkle with salt and pepper and cover with pats of butter.
- Place in preheated 500° oven uncovered for 5 minutes per pound. *Do not open oven door!* When roast has cooked required time, turn off oven and leave for 2 hours. Don't open oven door until end of time.
- When time is finished, you'll have a beautiful roast that is delicious served with a Brown Pecan Sauce. (Roast will not smoke if it's placed on a small rack and ½ cup water is added to pan.)

BROWN PECAN SAUCE
½ lb. butter, softened
1½ C. pecans, coarsely chopped
¼ C. Maker's Mark
⅛ C. spearmint leaves, chopped

- To prepare Brown Pecan Sauce, melt softened butter in skillet over high heat. Add pecans and cook until butter begins to darken and nuts start to brown.
- When butter ceases to foam, reduce heat and add bourbon and chopped mint leaves. Garnish with lemon wedges and sprigs of mint.

SKILLET SAUCED CHICKEN   *Serves 8*

"A recipe that's dedicated to the busy cook."

1 bottle Maker's Mark Gourmet Sauce
2 C. ginger ale
1 chicken, cut into serving pieces

- Mix first 2 ingredients together in cold electric skillet.
- Salt chicken, place into skillet, turning chicken 2-3 times to coat generously with sauce.
- Cover and cook at 350° for 30 minutes or until tender, turning occasionally. (May need to add water near end of cooking time.)
- Serve immediately.

WHITE BARBECUE SAUCE   *Yields 1 cup*

"This is an unusual basting sauce for grilled chicken or pork."

1 C. mayonnaise
3 Tbs. Maker's Mark
1 Tbs. orange juice, freshly squeezed
1 tsp. freshly ground pepper

- Combine ingredients, adding bourbon slowly and mixing well.
- Serve with your choice of meats.

WATER CHESTNUT SAUCE

Yields 2¹/₂ cups

"This sauce is very different and a wonderful addition to beef or chicken."

2 Tbs. drippings from roasting pan
1 (10½-ounce) can chicken broth
2 Tbs. soy sauce
2 Tbs. Maker's Mark
2 (5-ounce) cans water chestnuts, drained and sliced
3 Tbs. green onions, chopped
2 Tbs. pimento, chopped
1 Tbs. cornstarch
¼ C. cold water

- Drain excess drippings from roasting pan, leaving about 2 tablespoons. Stir in chicken broth, scraping pan to loosen particles.
- Transfer to saucepan and bring to a boil. Add soy sauce, bourbon, water chestnuts, onions, and pimento; simmer 5 minutes. Blend in cornstarch that has been dissolved in ¼ cup cold water.
- Cook, stirring constantly, until sauce thickens slightly. If seasonings are too strong in flavor, add extra water. (Extra cornstarch may be needed for thickening.)
- Serve in heated dish.

BERRY GLAZED HAM

Serves 16

"No one will ever guess that this is a 'precooked' or 'canned' ham. The extra cooking time and delicious sauce make the difference."

8 lbs. precooked ham or 5 lb. canned ham
1 C. cranberry sauce (whole berry)
3 Tbs. prepared mustard
1 C. brown sugar
½ C. orange juice concentrate, thawed
¼ C. Maker's Mark

- Combine cranberry sauce, mustard, brown sugar, orange juice concentrate, and bourbon.
- Coat ham with above sauce, cover with foil and bake at 350° for 2 hours. Baste ham with drippings in bottom of pan every 30 minutes.
- Allow ham to set about 1 hour before serving. (Have butcher slice ham before you cook it and it will be ready for instant serving.)

GREEN PEPPERCORN SAUCE

Yields 1¹/₂ cups

"A sauce that is popular served over broiled fish, grilled steaks, baked chicken, or pork – it dresses up any entrée."

3 Tbs. butter
3 Tbs. minced shallots
2-3 Tbs. Maker's Mark
2 Tbs. green peppercorns, rinsed and drained
1 bouillon cube, crushed
1 C. heavy cream
1 Tbs. butter, softened

- Melt butter in small saucepan; add shallots and sauté until golden.
- Stir in bourbon and reduce heat to low; add remaining ingredients, except butter, and cook until thickened, stirring constantly.
- Swirl in remaining butter and serve. (Sour cream or plain yogurt can be substituted for heavy cream.)

PERFECT ROAST LEG OF LAMB
Serves 8

*"This mint sauce goes well with any cut of lamb. When served warm,
the sauce is syrupy; when cool, it will thicken into a jelly."*

1 leg of lamb (approximately
   6 lbs.)
2 garlic cloves, minced
1 Tbs. paprika
1½ tsp. rosemary (dried)
1½ tsp. oregano (dried)

ORANGE BASTING SAUCE

¼ C. butter
1 (6-ounce) can frozen orange
   juice concentrate, thawed
¼ C. Maker's Mark

MINT JELLY SAUCE

¼ C. sugar
3 Tbs. Maker's Mark
⅓ C. water
1 (10-ounce) jar mint jelly
1 C. finely chopped fresh
   mint leaves

- Preheat oven to 350°; combine seasonings and press over entire leg of lamb.
- Insert meat thermometer and roast about 20 minutes per lb. or 140° for medium done. (Well done usually takes 30 to 35 minutes per lb.).
- While lamb is roasting, combine sauce ingredients and simmer uncovered for 15 minutes. After lamb has roasted 1 hour, baste frequently with sauce until meat is desired degree of doneness.
- Allow lamb to stand for 15 minutes before slicing and serve with Mint Jelly Sauce.
- To make mint sauce, mix first 3 ingredients together in saucepan over medium heat. When sugar dissolves, add jelly and simmer until jelly is completely melted.
- Add mint leaves and serve immediately with lamb.

BOURBON STEAK PASTA
Serves 8

*"This noodle accompaniment is the most often requested
side dish in my kitchen."*

½ C. brown sugar
10 ounces soy sauce
2 tsp. lemon juice
1 C. Maker's Mark
1½ C. water

SOUR CREAM NOODLES

1 (8-ounce) pkg. thin noodles
½ pt. sour cream
¾ C. grated Parmesan cheese

- Combine all ingredients in jar with tight fitting lid; shake well and store in refrigerator.
- To use sauce, pour over steaks and marinate 24 hours in refrigerator.
- Bring steaks to room temperature and grill over ash-gray coals, basting frequently with marinade.
- Serve accompanied by sour cream noodles.
- Cook noodles in salted water until slightly tender; drain, rinse with cold water.
- Mix noodles and sour cream. Add ½ cup Parmesan cheese, mix and put into buttered casserole.
- Sprinkle top lightly with remaining ¼ cup Parmesan cheese. Bake 1 hour at 225°.
- Leftover can be sliced in thin strips and added to leftover noodles for a lunch that's special!

PINEAPPLE BOURBON CHICKEN
Serves 4

"Bourbon sauce can enhance any choice of meat."

2 Tbs. olive oil

1 green pepper, cut into ¼-in. strips

4 skinned and boned chicken breasts, cut into ½-in. cubes

1 (8-ounce) can pineapple rings, drained and cut into bite-size pieces

½ C. almonds

BOURBON SAUCE

½ C. chicken broth

⅓ C. reserve syrup from pineapple (add water if needed to make required amount)

3 Tbs. Maker's Mark

1 Tbs. cornstarch dissolved in ⅛ C. cold water

2 Tbs. orange marmalade

1 Tbs. soy sauce

1 tsp. grated ginger root

- Heat oil in wok and stir-fry green pepper 1-2 minutes. Push aside.
- Stir-fry chicken 3-4 minutes until done. Return green peppers to chicken cubes, adding pineapple and almonds.
- Combine sauce ingredients and add to wok. Heat and stir until sauce is thickened and clear.
- Serve immediately with cooked rice, if desired.

"STARRED" WALNUT CHICKEN
Serves 6

"Out of this world – what more can I say."

6 large (half) chicken breasts, boned and skinned

Salt and pepper to taste

2 egg whites

1 C. finely chopped walnuts

2 Tbs. Maker's Mark

LIME SAUCE

2 Tbs. butter

2 Tbs. flour

1 C. chicken broth

¼ tsp. salt

⅛ tsp. white pepper

2 egg yolks

2 whole eggs

½ tsp. grated lime peel

2 Tbs. fresh lime juice

- Soak nuts overnight in bourbon.
- Season chicken with salt and pepper. Beat egg whites lightly; dip chicken in egg whites, coating generously.
- Drain well, then cover with soaked walnuts. Place in buttered baking dish, bake at 350° for 20-25 minutes, just until chicken is cooked.
- To make Lime Sauce, melt butter and stir in flour; add chicken broth, salt and white pepper. Cook, stirring, until mixture boils for 1 minute.
- Beat together egg yolks and whole eggs.
- Stir hot sauce into eggs, stirring quickly. Return mixture to very low heat, stirring constantly, until thickened.
- Remove from heat and blend in lime peel and juice. Serve chicken with Lime Sauce.

GOURMET BEEF BRISKET

*"Leftovers from this dish are great and will keep for several days.
Terrific for serving large crowds."*

6-8 lbs. lean beef brisket,
   deboned and flat (not rolled)
½ bottle liquid hickory smoke
½ tsp. each garlic, onion, and
   celery salt
1 small bottle Worcestershire
   sauce
Salt and pepper to taste
1 bottle Maker's Mark Gourmet
   Sauce

- Night before cooking, place meat in large, long shallow pan; cover generously with liquid smoke and sprinkle with garlic, onion, and celery salt on both sides of meat. Cover and refrigerate.
- Next morning saturate meat with Worcestershire sauce, salt, and pepper. Cover top of pan with foil, folding over edge of pan.
- Roast in 275° oven for 5 hours; remove from oven and take off foil.
- Cover meat with bottle of Maker's Mark Gourmet Sauce; return to oven (uncovered) and roast 1 hour.
- Remove again from oven and lift meat from sauce to platter allowing to cool before slicing. Place sauce in cool place so grease will rise to top and then skim off grease.
- Thicken remaining sauce with small amount corn-starch; serve over cool, sliced beef.
- Additional Gourmet Sauce can be added to base sauce in which meat was cooked to make more gravy.
- Serve on sliced eggrolls, or sliced on plate.

HANDCRAFTED BARBECUE SAUCE

"Great with chicken or ribs!"

1 medium onion, chopped
   (approximately ½ C.)
½ C. molasses
½ C. catsup
2 tsp. orange peel, finely
   shredded
⅓ C. orange juice (freshly
   squeezed)
2 Tbs. olive oil
1 Tbs. vinegar
1 Tbs. steak sauce
½ tsp. prepared mustard
½ tsp. Worcestershire sauce
¼ tsp. each garlic powder, salt,
   cayenne pepper, hot sauce
⅛ tsp. ground cloves
¼ C. Maker's Mark

- Combine all ingredients, except bourbon, and cook over low heat for 30 minutes or until onions are transparent.
- Add bourbon and simmer for 10 minutes.
- Use as a barbecue sauce.

GRILLED STEAK WITH HORSERADISH SAUCE

Serves 4

"This inexpensive cut of beef is also tasty served as a hot appetizer."

2 lbs. flank steak
2 Tbs. olive oil
1 tsp. each of sage and
   rosemary
1 Tbs. lemon juice
¼ C. Maker's Mark
¼ tsp. garlic powder

- Place flank steak in baking dish and rub all over with oil. Crush sage and rosemary and rub herbs on both sides of meat.

- Sprinkle lemon juice and bourbon on both sides also. Dust with garlic powder. Put steak aside to marinate for 3 hours, turning several times while marinating.

- Cook steaks over a hot grill for about 2 minutes, brush with marinade, and turn over to grill second side for no longer than 2 minutes. Meat will be medium rare.

- Remove to a carving board and let stand for 15 minutes. Cut across the grain at an angle to produce long, thin strips; meat must be cut thin. Serve on warm plates with horseradish sauce.

HORSERADISH SAUCE

2 Tbs. flour
⅛ tsp. pepper
1¼ Tbs. prepared horseradish
¼ tsp. sugar
1 C. sour cream
1 C. beef stock

- For sauce, blend all ingredients into beef stock and stir vigorously. Cook over medium heat until it bubbles, stirring constantly. Sauce can be served hot or cold.

PRIME RIB IN ROCK SALT

Serves 8

"There is a secret to always serving superb beef. First, buy only the very best and properly aged beef. Second, cover entire roast with rock salt and start cooking in a hot oven."

4 lbs. prime rib roast
2 Tbs. Worcestershire sauce
1 tsp. garlic powder
1 tsp. paprika
½ teaspoon each of salt and
   pepper
Rock salt, enough to form paste
   over roast
¼ C. Maker's Mark

- Preheat oven to 475°.

- Combine all ingredients except rock salt and bourbon in small bowl; rub into roast.

- Cover entire roast with a thick coating of rock salt, moistened with water. Be sure to form a thick crust (1½ in. thick).

- Start roast in 475° oven immediately after salting. This fuses the salt and keeps the juices in. Roast for 12-13 minutes per pound (medium rare).

- Break salt from roast with wooden mallet. Salt will come off in large sheets, and will not impart saltiness to roast.

- Before serving, brush roast with generous amount of bourbon. Heat remaining bourbon, ignite, and pour over roast. Roast should flame.

MARINATED PORK LOIN WITH ORANGE SAUCE — *Serves 8*

"What a special way to serve pork, and festive enough for any dinner party."

5 lbs. pork loin

MARINADE

½ C. lemon juice
¼ C. soy sauce
½ C. orange juice
¼ C. Maker's Mark
½ tsp. pressed garlic
2 tsp. ground ginger

ORANGE SAUCE

½ C. sugar
½ tsp. cinnamon
1 Tbs. grated orange rind
16 whole cloves, tied in
    cheesecloth bag
1 Tbs. cornstarch
½ tsp. salt
½ C. orange juice
½ C. Maker's Mark
10 mandarin orange slices
    (canned variety), cut
    into halves

- Combine marinade ingredients and pour over pork; cover and refrigerate overnight, turning occasionally.
- Remove meat from refrigerator and reserve marinade for basting.
- Roast at 350° for approximately 2½ hours or until meat registers 185° on meat thermometer. While roast is cooking, baste often with marinade.
- Prepare orange sauce by combining all ingredients, except oranges, cooking over a medium heat until sauce is thickened and clear, stirring constantly. Remove bag of cloves and add orange slices.
- Serve by arranging meat on serving plate and pouring orange sauce over meat.

STEAK AU POIVRE — *Serves 4*

"For a thinner sauce, substitute beef broth for heavy cream."

2½ lbs. steak, 1½ inches thick
    (porterhouse, sirloin, or
    Delmonico)
3 Tbs. whole black
    peppercorns
¼ tsp. salt
¼ C. olive oil
¼ C. Maker's Mark
½ pt. heavy cream
1 Tbs. minced parsley

- Coarsely crush peppercorns using a mortar and pestle or bottom of small skillet.
- Trim excess fat from steak, season and pound peppercorns into both sides until meat is thickly coated. Coat meat 2 hours before cooking.
- Heat olive oil to smoking point in heavy skillet and broil steak to desired doneness on both sides. Remove to heated platter.
- Discard all but 2 tablespoons of drippings, add bourbon, heat and flame for about 1 minute. Lower temperature and blend in cream until heated through. When sauce thickens, pour over steaks and garnish with parsley.

BOURBON-BUTTERED CORNISH HENS – CRANBERRY PECAN STUFFING

Serves 6

"Baste the hens regularly so they will be juicy – what a delightful glaze for turkey too. Stuffing has lots of ingredients that combine for an outstanding flavor."

6 (1 lb.) Cornish hens
Salt and pepper for seasoning
½ C. butter, melted
¼ C. honey
½ C. Maker's Mark

- Remove giblets from hens and reserve for another use. Rinse hens with cold water, pat dry. Sprinkle cavity of each with salt and pepper.

- Place hens, breast side up in shallow baking pan; use ¼ cup melted butter for the first basting of hens; bake at 350° for 1-1½ hours (test for doneness.)

- Combine the remaining ¼ cup butter, honey and bourbon; brush on hens every 15 minutes of cooking time until hens are tender.

- Serve with Cranberry Pecan Stuffing.

CRANBERRY PECAN STUFFING

6 slices bacon
1 C. sliced celery
½ C. onion, chopped
1 (8½-ounce) pkg. herb-
  seasoned stuffing mix
1½ C. cooked wild rice
¾ C. raw cranberries, chopped
¾ C. walnuts
1 can (10½-ounce) condensed
  beef broth
1 egg, slightly beaten
4 Tbs. Maker's Mark

- In skillet, cook bacon until crisp; drain and crumble. Pour off all but 2 tablespoons drippings.

- Cook celery and onion in drippings until tender. Combine celery, onion, stuffing mix, cooked rice, cranberries, walnuts, broth and egg. After mixing thoroughly, add bourbon. If stuffing is dry, add more bourbon or water.

- Bake in a round casserole at 350° for 30 minutes or make into balls using ice cream scoop; line casserole with balls, baking for 20 minutes. *(I don't stuff birds.)*

- Serve with Candied Orange Shells and Spiked Cranberries.

GLAZED CANADIAN BACON

Serves 8

"This dish is perfect for a 'before the races' brunch."

2 lbs. Canadian bacon,
  casing removed
½ C. water
3 Tbs. Maker's Mark
2 Tbs. apricot preserves
2 tsp. dry mustard
⅛ tsp. ground ginger
⅛ tsp. salt

- Place bacon on rack in shallow baking pan.

- Heat remaining ingredients to boiling, then remove from heat.

- Roast bacon at 350°, basting frequently with glazing mixture, for 1 hour..

- Slice bacon; heat remaining glaze and serve with meat.

BEEF WITH BLACK PEPPERCORNS

Serves 8

"Very spicy, but everyone thinks this recipe's a winner!"

4 ½ lbs. beef tenderloin,
  trimmed
Salt to taste
1 C. black peppercorns,
  crushed
8 Tbs. unsalted butter
½ C. Maker's Mark

- Preheat oven to 550°.
- Season beef with salt, then roll in crushed peppercorns.
- Melt 2 Tbs. butter over high heat in roasting pan. Add beef and sear on all sides. Roast in 550° oven for 30 minutes, turning once after 15 minutes.
- Then place beef on underside of a small plate inverted onto a large plate. (This allows beef to rest without sitting in its juices.) Cover with foil and place in oven with heat OFF and door ajar. Let stand 1 hour.
- Discard fat in pan, reserving juices. Add bourbon and deglaze over low heat. Remove beef from plate and pour collected juices into roasting pan.
- Stir over low heat until thoroughly warmed. Turn off heat, add remaining butter that has been cut into small pieces.
- Carve beef. Arrange slices on platter and serve with above sauce.

LOBSTER AND MAKER'S

Serves 2

"Shrimp can be used instead of lobster for an equally delicious dish."

2 (1½-lbs. each) lobsters
⅛ C. clarified butter
5 shallots, minced
2 Tbs. chives, minced
2 tsp. fresh parsley, chopped
½ C. heavy cream
¼ C. Maker's Mark
Salt and pepper to taste
Rice pilaf (made in advance)
Lemon for garnish

- Plunge lobsters into boiling water and cook for 1-2 minutes or until shells turn red; chill.
- Remove meat from tail and claws, leaving shell intact for serving.
- Saute shallots, chives, and parsley in clarified butter for 1 minute. Add lobster, cream, and whisky; heat thoroughly, but *do not boil.* Season with salt and pepper.
- In lobster shell, add a bed of rice pilaf and top with lobster; garnish with additional chopped parsley and lemon, if desired.

APPLE-GLAZED PORK TENDERLOIN   *Serves 4*

"One pound of boned pork will serve 2 to 3; but allow ¾ lb. of bone-in pork for 1 person."

2 whole pork tenderloins (each about ¾ lb.)

MARINADE
½ C. Maker's Mark
¾ C. apple cider
¼ C. brown sugar (packed)
¼ tsp. ground cinnamon

BOURBON APPLESAUCE
3 Red Delicious apples, diced
1 onion, diced
3 ounces Maker's Mark
1 C. chicken broth
1 C. beef broth
3 ounces heavy cream
¼ C. walnuts (chopped)

- Place pork tenderloin in glass baking dish. Thoroughly mix bourbon, cider, brown sugar, cinnamon and pour over tenderloin.
- Cover dish with plastic wrap and refrigerate 8 hours or more, turning meat several times.
- Heat oven to 325°. Place marinated tenderloin in oven and cook 1 hour 15 minutes or until internal temperature of meat is 170°. Brush meat with marinade every 15-20 minutes. Once meat is done, let it stand out of oven 10-15 minutes before carving.
- To prepare bourbon applesauce, sauté apples and onions for 5 minutes until soft. Add bourbon, flambé, being careful not to have bourbon near flame when pouring.
- Add broths to other ingredients and simmer for 5 minutes. Then add cream and reduce sauce until it begins to thicken; whirl in blender to make smooth, if desired.
- Add walnuts to sauce and serve with tenderloin.

BOURBON SHRIMP   *Serves 4*

"This recipe can be used as an appetizer or an entrée."

3 Tbs. butter (no substitute)
1 lb. shrimp (20–26 count), peeled and deveined
¼ C. Maker's Mark
¼ C. heavy cream
¼ tsp. salt

- Melt butter in skillet; add shrimp and sauté until pink and firm (Do not overcook).
- Splash shrimp with bourbon; remove to serving dish and keep warm.
- Add cream to skillet, scraping bottom of pan with spoon as you mix; add salt. Heat mixture over medium heat and pour over shrimp.
- Serve immediately.

FLAMED STUFFED CROWN PORK
Serves 8

"Have butcher make crown roast at market. At bottom of roast, cut slits between ribs so roast will carve easily."

1 (12–16 rib) crown pork roast
  (7–8 lbs.)
Salt and pepper to taste
1 large red onion
¼ C. butter, melted
4 large fresh mushrooms,
  sliced
2 cooking apples, peeled
  and diced
3 C. herb-seasoned stuffing
  mix
1 C. applesauce
3 Tbs. Maker's Mark
1 (10-ounce) jar apricot
  preserves
½ C. Maker's Mark

- Season roast with salt and pepper, bone ends up on rack in shallow roasting pan. Insert meat thermometer without touching fat or bone.
- Sauté onion in butter until tender; add mushrooms, cook, stirring constantly, until tender. Add apples and cook 1 minute, stirring constantly.
- Stir in next 3 ingredients; spoon stuffing into center of roast and cover with foil.
- Bake roast at 325° for 2 hours or until thermometer registers 160°.
- Heat preserves and only ¼ C. bourbon, basting roast with this mixture every 10 minutes after 1 hour. (Use only ¾ of this mixture for basting).
- Remove from oven and let stand 15 minutes; place on serving platter.
- Heat reserved basting mixture again and remove from heat. Pour remaining ¼ C. bourbon over heated preserves mixture, ignite, and pour over roast.

BOTTLE BARBECUED RIBS
Serves 4

"Ribs may be cooked in a Dutch oven for 30 minutes and then grilled over slow coals for 45 minutes."

3½ – 4 lbs. ribs (pork or beef)
½ tsp. garlic salt
¼ tsp. pepper
2 C. Maker's Mark Gourmet
  Sauce

- Cut ribs into serving size pieces. Place ribs, meaty side up in shallow roasting pan; sprinkle with garlic salt and pepper.
- Roast for 1 hour at 350°, drain off excess fat.
- Brush ribs with 1½ C. Maker's Mark Gourmet Sauce and roast for 15 minutes at 325°.
- Add rest of sauce to meat and roast 15 minutes longer or until done. Baste well with sauce during roasting.

BLACKENED FISH

"This cooking process produces smoke, but iron skillet can be heated to red hot inside and then moved to outside grill or hot plate."

1 tsp. each of red pepper, white pepper, black pepper, and cayenne pepper

2 tsp. marjoram

1 tsp. onion salt

2 tsp. garlic salt

¼ C. melted butter

2 orange roughy fillets

LEMON TARTAR SAUCE

(Combine following ingredients and serve.)

Juice of 1 lemon

1 C. mayonnaise

¼ C. minced green onions

¼ C. chopped fresh parsley

1 Tbs. Maker's Mark Gourmet Sauce

- Mix dry seasonings in small bowl.

- Heat a large cast-iron skillet over very high heat until it's beyond the smoking stage and you see white ash in skillet bottom (at least 10 minutes).

- Brush 1 side of fillets with butter, sprinkle with seasonings. Place seasoned side down in skillet; cook for 5 minutes.

- Brush unseasoned side of fillets with butter, sprinkle with seasonings and turn fillets over. Cook for 4 minutes longer. Fish will be crisp and black on outside.

- Serve with lemon tartar sauce.

- If you're in a hurry, buy prepared cajun seasoning and use instead of above herb mixture. Also this method of cooking is great for steaks and pork chops!

SHISH-KABOBS (THE SOUTHERN WAY)

"These savory meat chunks are easy party fare when skewers are threaded early in the day and refrigerated until needed."

3 lbs. sirloin steak cut into 1½ x 1½ in. cubes

1 clove garlic, crushed

4 Tbs. soy sauce

1 tsp. each salt and pepper

½ C. lemon juice

⅓ C. Maker's Mark

¾ C. ginger ale

2 Tbs. sugar

Onions, green peppers, mushrooms and tomatoes, cut into pieces

- Combine marinade ingredients and mix well.

- Place meat cubes in container, cover with marinade and allow to stand at room temperature for 2 hours or refrigerate overnight.

- Skewer meat alternately with onions, mushrooms, peppers and tomatoes.

- Grill over charcoal or under broiler until medium rare and serve immediately.

KENTUCKY BEEF WELLINGTON
Serves 16

*"Don't be overcome by the detailed instructions. This is an extremely
easy dish to prepare, but it's impressive to serve."*

1 (7-lb.) beef tenderloin,
  trimmed
1 (8-ounce) pkg. liverwurst
  spread
1 C. fresh mushrooms,
  chopped
3 Tbs. Maker's Mark
1 (16-ounce) pkg. frozen puff
  pastry, thawed
1 egg yolk
1 Tbs. milk
Parsley for garnish

- Place tenderloin on rack in shallow roasting pan. Bake uncovered, at 425° for 25–30 minutes; remove from oven, and let stand 30 minutes.
- Combine liverwurst spread, mushrooms, and bourbon; set aside.
- Roll pastry to a 14x20-inch rectangle on lightly floured surface. Spread ⅓ of liverwurst mixture over top of beef and then place it, top side down, in middle of pastry.
- Spread remaining liverwurst mixture over sides of tenderloin. Bring sides of pastry up, and overlap to form a seam, trimming off excess pastry. Seal tenderloin at all edges; invert roast.
- Combine egg yolk and milk; brush evenly over pastry. Make decorative designs from left over pastry, if desired, and also brush with milk mixture.
- Bake, uncovered, in lightly greased 9x13-inch pan at 425° for 30-40 minutes. Let stand 15 minutes before slicing. Garnish with parsley.

SPICY BARBECUED BEEF
Serves 10

*"A slow cooker may be used to prepare this dish. Just cook on low 10–12
hours or until beef is tender; drain and then add Gourmet Sauce."*

1 (5–6 lb.) rump roast
2 medium onions, sliced
4–5 whole cloves
1 bottle Maker's Mark Gourmet
  Sauce
⅛ tsp. hot sauce
Hamburger buns (optional)

- Cover roast with water in large Dutch oven. Add onion and cloves; cover and cook over medium heat 3 hours or until beef is tender.
- Drain meat, shred with a fork, add Gourmet Sauce and hot sauce to Dutch oven. Cover and cook over low heat 30 minutes, stirring occasionally.
- Serve on buns or over rice as a main course.

ELEGANT STEAKBURGERS WITH BLEU CHEESE

*"The egg whites help hold the shape of the burgers
and also keep them moist."*

2 lbs. ground chuck
½ C. fresh mushrooms,
    chopped
½ tsp. soy sauce
1 tsp. Worcestershire sauce
¼ tsp. each of seasoned salt
    and pepper
1 tsp. Maker's Mark
2 egg whites (slightly beaten)

- Combine all ingredients together, mixing well.
- Form patties and refrigerate 2 hours before cooking.
- Grill burgers until desired doneness is reached.

BLEU CHEESE SPREAD

4 Tbs. cream cheese
2 Tbs. finely chopped onions
3 Tbs. bleu cheese
3 Tbs. plain yogurt
⅛ tsp. white pepper
1-2 Tbs. Maker's Mark

- Combine bleu cheese spread ingredients. After burgers have cooked, spread with cheese spread mixture, and slip under broiler just long enough to heat cheese.
- This bleu cheese spread is also great served on steaks.

SHRIMP SAMUELS

Serves 6

*"Allow ¾–1 lb. per person when buying unpeeled shrimp to serve
as a main dish."*

¾ lb. butter (3 sticks)
¼ lb. brown sugar
2 Tbs. fresh thyme
1 Tbs. fresh rosemary
½ tsp. Tabasco
1 Tbs. Worcestershire sauce
1 Tbs. minced garlic
24 large shrimp, unpeeled
1 Tbs. fresh lemon juice
Salt and pepper to taste
¼ tsp. cayenne pepper
4 ounces Maker's Mark

- Melt butter in large skillet; add brown sugar, thyme, rosemary, Tabasco, Worcestershire sauce, and garlic. Sauté for 2 minutes.
- Add shrimp and cook until pink (3 minutes).
- Add rest of ingredients, flame, and simmer for 2 minutes.
- Serve on bed of rice.

CANDIED ORANGE SHELLS FILLED WITH SPIKED CRANBERRIES

"Candied orange peel has a holiday fragrance – and the cranberries contain that quality spirit!"

5 small navel oranges
4 C. water
2 C. sugar

SPIKED CRANBERRIES
1 C. water
½ C. sugar
12-ounce pkg. fresh cranberries
⅓ C. candied ginger, cut in strips
2 Tbs. Maker's Mark

- Halve and hollow out oranges – cut large strip off bottom of each half so it will stand upright.
- Combine water and sugar in heavy saucepan and bring to boil. Cook until sugar dissolves; add orange shells and poach gently for 10 minutes.
- Drain oranges and allow to cool; fill with cranberry mixture.
- Combine water and sugar in heavy sauce, bring to boil and cook until sugar dissolves.
- Selectively pick over cranberries, disregarding faulty ones, and add to sugar mixture. Bring to a boil, reduce heat and simmer for 5 minutes.
- Remove from heat and stir in candied ginger and bourbon.

GRILLED PORK CHOPS WITH BOURBON BASTING SAUCE   *Serves 4*

"A southern summertime treat."

2 Tbs. butter
½ C. soy sauce
1 lemon
½ tsp. onion salt
⅛ tsp. freshly ground pepper
¼ tsp. Tabasco
2 Tbs. Maker's Mark
4 pork chops, each 1-inch thick

- In small saucepan, mix butter, soy sauce, lemon (cut in half, squeeze juice in, and drop shells in), onion salt, pepper, Tabasco, and bourbon. Boil 5 minutes.
- Cook pork chops on grill and baste often with sauce the last half hour of cooking.
- Remaining sauce can be served with chops.

OYSTER AND MUSHROOM CASSEROLE

Serves 8

"Try this dish on your next holiday buffet table."

½ C. butter
1 lb. fresh mushrooms
6 Tbs. flour
3 C. oyster liquid and evaporated milk, combined to equal required amount
1 qt. oysters, drained
1 tsp. salt
½ tsp. each of paprika and nutmeg
2 Tbs. Maker's Mark
1 C. bread crumbs

- Melt ¼ C. of butter in saucepan; add mushrooms and sauté for 3 minutes.

- Remove mushrooms, and melt the remainder of butter in same saucepan. Add flour and stir over low heat until blended.

- Add combined oyster-cream liquid slowly, stirring constantly until sauce is thick and boiling. Add mushrooms and bring to a boil again.

- Add oysters, blending into mixture, taking care not to burn. Add salt, paprika, nutmeg, bourbon stirring into mixture.

- Pour mixture into casserole scattering bread crumbs over top. Dot with butter.

- Shortly before serving, place casserole in oven until heated through (350°) and bread crumbs are brown.

BARBECUED SHRIMP

Serves 4

"A super easy and delicious dish."

½ C. butter
¾ C. Maker's Mark Gourmet Sauce
2 Tbs. lemon juice
¼ tsp. black pepper
2 lbs. unshelled (medium–large) shrimp
⅓ C. Maker's Mark

- Turn on broiler and melt butter in a broiler (9x13-inch) pan. Remove from oven and stir in Gourmet Sauce, lemon juice, and pepper.

- Add shrimp, toss to coat, and spread out in pan.

- Broil 5 inches from heat for 4 minutes; turn shrimp and broil 4 minutes longer. Serve while hot; sprinkle with bourbon.

■ *Unique Pies*　　　　■ *Pastries*　　　　■ *Distinctive Cookies*

During the fermenting period, the special strain of Maker's Mark yeast goes to work to convert the sugars in the grains to alcohol.

This is called the "fermenting" period, and the mash in the large vats have all the characteristics of something simmering on the stove... although there is no heat applied. The mash "ferments" for 96 hours and when the process is complete you have what is called "distiller's beer."

At this point, the distiller's beer enters the still near the top. Steam is injected from the low side of the still and rises through the mash, carrying the vapors to the top of the five-story-high, copper still. The vapors are then distilled off into "unfinished" whisky. Visitors can see this clear, pure whisky as it comes off the still in what's called the "Tail Box."

Opposite side photo: (left to right) Coconut Cream Splash Pie, Mystery Cherry Pie, Assortment of the Maker's Cookies

KENTUCKY MINT JULEP PIE

"This pie crust has Mint Julep Creme Candies added to the traditional cookie crust – what an addition!"

2 envelopes unflavored gelatin

2 C. light cream (half and half)

¼ C. granulated sugar

½ tsp. salt

1½ Tbs. green crème de menthe

1 Tbs. Maker's Mark

4 egg whites

1 C. heavy cream

MINT JULEP CREME CRUST

1¼ C. crushed chocolate wafer

1⅓ C. Mint Julep Creme Candies, finely chopped

6 Tbs. butter, melted

- Prepare pie shell (see below).

- For filling, sprinkle gelatin over ½ cup light cream; let stand 5 minutes to soften. Stir over low heat until gelatin is completely dissolved.

- Add sugar, salt, remaining light cream, crème de menthe and bourbon; cook, stirring constantly, until sugar dissolves and mixture is well blended.

- Remove from heat; refrigerate mixture 30 minutes.

- Beat egg whites until stiff peaks form.

- In large bowl with mixer at high speed, beat heavy cream until stiff peaks form. With wooden spoon, gently stir beaten whites into cream; gradually add gelatin mixture, stirring gently and blending thoroughly.

- Refrigerate about 45 minutes and then swirl attractively into pie shell.

- Make *Mint Julep Creme Crust* by combining crumbs and candy in bowl; pour melted butter over mixture and blend till crumbs are moistened. Butter bottom of 9-inch pie pan (not sides because shell may fall during baking) and gently press crumbs evenly over bottom and sides of pan. Bake in preheated 350° oven for 8 minutes. Let crust cool to room temperature before filling.

SOUTHERN PECAN BOURBON PIE

"My very favorite pie, absolutely."

6 eggs, well beaten

1 C. butter, creamed

⅓ C. granulated sugar

1½ C. light corn syrup

2 C. chopped pecans

6 Tbs. Maker's Mark

2 tsp. vanilla

1 (9-in.) unbaked deep pie shell

Whipped cream for garnish

- Preheat oven to 450°.

- In a bowl combine butter and eggs, mix well. Add remaining ingredients and pour into unbaked pie shell.

- Bake at 450° for 10 minutes; lower oven to 300° and bake 30 minutes more.

- Serve warm and garnish with whipped cream.

MYSTERY CHERRY PIE

*"This lattice pie is enhanced by the addition of cranberries and bourbon.
The ingredients are a surprise to everyone."*

1 C. granulated sugar
⅓ C. all-purpose flour
½ tsp. ground cinnamon
¼ tsp. salt
2 (16½-ounce) cans pitted
    sweet cherries in heavy
    syrup, well drained, but
    reserve syrup
⅓ C. reserved cherry syrup
2 Tbs. Maker's Mark
1 (12-ounce) pkg. cranberries,
    fresh or frozen

FLAKY PIE CRUST

3 C. flour
½ C. butter
¾ C. shortening
1 egg, slightly beaten
1 tsp. each of vinegar, sugar
    and salt
5½ Tbs. cold water

■ Prepare Flaky Pie Crust (bottom and top for lattice –
    see below).

■ Combine sugar, flour, cinnamon and salt in large
    saucepan; stir in cherry syrup and bourbon.

■ Stir mixture over medium heat until sugar is melted;
    add cranberries. Cook 5–8 minutes, stirring frequently
    until mixture is thickened and bubbling.

■ Remove from heat; stir in cherries. Let stand about 45
    minutes until completely cool, stirring occasionally.

■ Heat oven to 425° and pour cooled filling into pre-
    pared crust. Arrange reserved strips of dough over
    filling in lattice pattern, trim strips to match lower crust
    overhang. Crimp edges.

■ Bake 25–30 minutes until filling is bubbly and crust is
    golden brown.

■ Cool on rack and serve hot.

■ Prepare *Flaky Pie Crust* by cutting shortening into
    flour, adding sugar and salt. Make well in dry ingredi-
    ents and add egg, water and vinegar which has been
    mixed together. This makes 4 crusts. Sticks of dough
    will keep in refrigerator for 3 days or you can freeze it
    for later use.

SPIKED CANDY PIE
Serves 8

*"Everyone loves this pie. It's always festive using either flavor of Maker's
Mark Candies — Bourbon Chocolates or Mint Julep Cremes."*

4 egg yolks
⅓ C. sugar
⅛ tsp. salt
2 tsp. plain gelatin
2 Tbs. water
1 C. cream, whipped stiff
2 Tbs. Maker's Mark
4 ounces Maker's Mark
    Bourbon Creme Candies,
    coarsely chopped

PRETZEL CRUST

¾ C. pretzel crumbs
⅓ C. butter, melted
3 Tbs. sugar

■ Prepare *Pretzel Crust* (see below).

■ Beat egg yolks until light; add sugar and salt.

■ Mix plain gelatin with water and melt over hot water.
    Add to yolk mixture along with whipped cream, and
    bourbon.

■ Cool slightly and pour into pie shell. Cover with
    4 ounces of candy, coarsely chopped. Allow to stand
    in refrigerator for 4 hours to set before serving.

■ Prepare *Pretzel Crust* by combining crushed pretzels
    and melted butter with sugar. Press into bottom and
    sides of a 9-inch pie plate. Chill or freeze until needed.

■ Ordering information for candy is available in the
    Index Section.

FREEZER CHOCOLATE MOCHA PIE

Serves 8

"Chocolate, bourbon and coffee flavors combine for a fabulous pie. Keep this pie in your freezer for spontaneous entertaining."

6 (1-ounce) squares semi-sweet
   chocolate
½ tsp. instant coffee granules
2 eggs, beaten
3 Tbs. Maker's Mark
¼ C. confectioners' sugar
¾ C. whipping cream
1 tsp. vanilla extract

PECAN CRUST
_____

2 C. pecans, coarsely chopped
⅓ C. firmly packed brown
   sugar
3 Tbs. butter, melted
2 tsp. Maker's Mark

PECAN CREME
_____

¾ C. whipping cream
1 Tbs. Maker's Mark
½ C. pecans, chopped
Grated chocolate (for garnish)

- Prepare nut crust (see below).
- For filling, place chocolate squares and instant coffee granules in top of double boiler; bring to boil, then reduce heat to low and cook until chocolate melts.
- Gradually stir about ¼ melted chocolate into eggs, mixing well; add to remaining chocolate in double boiler.
- Slowly stir in bourbon and sugar. Cook, stirring constantly until mixture reaches 165°. Cool.
- Beat ¾ cup whipping cream until soft peaks form; fold into chocolate mixture. Stir in vanilla; spoon mixture into crust. Cover and freeze.
- Prepare *Pecan Crust* by combining all crust ingredients, mixing well. Firmly press mixture evenly over bottom and up sides of 9-inch pie plate. Bake at 350° for 10–12 minutes. Press sides of crust with back of wooden spoon.
- Prepare *Pecan Creme* garnish by beating ¾ C. whipping cream until foamy; gradually add 1 Tbs. bourbon, beating until stiff peaks form. Fold in pecans, dollop around edge of pie and sprinkle with grated chocolate.
- To serve, transfer pie from freezer to refrigerator 1 hour before serving.

MAKER'S SPECIAL WALNUT PIE

Serves 10

"This pie is so delicious, I always make two (so I can freeze one). Pie is traditionally served with vanilla ice cream and whipped cream."

½ C. sugar
¼ C. butter, melted
1 C. dark corn syrup
¼ C. Maker's Mark
1 tsp. vanilla
¼ tsp. salt
3 eggs, slightly beaten
1 (6-ounce) pkg. semi-sweet
   chocolate pieces
1 C. walnut halves or pieces
1 (9-in.) unbaked pie shell

- Preheat oven to 375°
- Beat first 7 ingredients together on electric mixer until well blended. Stir in chocolate chips and walnuts.
- Pour into pastry-lined pie plate. Cover edges with foil to prevent excessive browning; remove foil last 10 minutes of baking.
- Bake until set, in preheated 375° oven for 40–45 minutes.
- Cool and serve, or cover and refrigerate until serving time. Pie is best when gently heated before serving.

ICE CREAM MERINGUE PIE   Serves 8

*"The meringue crust can be used with other filling flavors. As you read
these pie recipes, you'll notice I have suggested lots of different crusts —
and special crusts do give an elegant touch."*

3 egg whites
½ tsp. baking powder
¾ C. granulated sugar
Pinch of salt
1 C. chocolate wafer crumbs
½ C. chopped pecans
1 tsp. vanilla extract
1 quart vanilla or coffee ice
  cream, softened
1 C. whipping cream
¼ C. confectioners' sugar
Sweet chocolate shavings for
  garnish
½ C. Maker's Mark

- For pie shell, beat egg whites until frothy; always use whites that are room temperature. Add baking powder, beating slightly. Gradually add sugar and salt; continue beating until stiff peaks form.

- Fold in chocolate wafer crumbs, pecans and vanilla. Spoon into buttered 9-inch pie plate, forming shell; swirl sides high and bake at 350° for 30 minutes, then cool.

- Spread ice cream evenly over meringue crust; cover and freeze 8 hours.

- Beat whipping cream until foamy; slowly add sugar, beating well until soft peaks form. Spread over frozen ice cream pie.

- Garnish with chocolate shavings; cover and freeze until firm again.

- Serve by allowing pie to stand at room temperature 10 minutes before slicing.

- Pour 1 tablespoon of bourbon over each serving.

SWEET POTATO PIE   Serves 8

*"What a true southern tradition pie! Serve instead of pumpkin pie on
Thanksgiving Day."*

1 C. boiled mashed sweet
  potatoes
1½ C. butter
1 C. granulated sugar
2 eggs
2 Tbs. lemon juice
¼ C. Maker's Mark
¼ tsp. mace

SPICED NUT CRUST
1 C. all-purpose flour
½ C. finely chopped pecans
¼ C. firmly packed brown
  sugar
6 Tbs. butter, melted
½ tsp. ground cinnamon

- Prepare nut crust (see below).

- Boil potatoes in water to cover until well done; peel and mash.

- For filling, cream butter and sugar. Add potatoes, eggs, lemon juice, bourbon and mace.

- Pour into slightly baked crust and bake at 375° for 40–50 minutes, until set in middle.

- Prepare *Spiced Nut Crust* by combining ingredients; stir well. Press onto bottom and sides of 9-inch pie plate. Bake crust only for 10 minutes in preheated 350° oven and this will prevent sweet potato mixture making crust soggy.

MINCEMEAT PIE TARTS

Serves 6

"This sweet tart crust is one of my favorites. It is also wonderful for strawberry pie — so sweet and delicate."

2 C. prepared mincemeat
1 C. chopped apple
1 C. chopped walnuts
2 Tbs. Maker's Mark

SWEET TART SHELLS

1 C. flour
2 Tbs. confectioners' sugar
1 stick margarine, melted

BOURBON SAUCE

⅓ C. granulated sugar
⅓ C. light brown sugar, firmly packed
1 C. water
1 lemon wedge
1 orange wedge
½ C. Maker's Mark

- For filling, combine mincemeat, apple, walnuts and bourbon in saucepan. Cook over medium heat until apples are tender. (Ingredients can be microwaved in glass casserole on high for 6–7 minutes.) Allow to cool.
- Prepare *Sweet Tart Shells* by mixing flour, sugar and melted margarine together in bowl; press to shape in tart pans. Bake for 8 minutes at 400°.
- Fill tart shells with mincemeat filling and serve warm with *Sauce*.
- For *Sauce* combine sugars with water; cook over medium heat, stirring until sugars are dissolved. Add lemon and orange wedges; bring to boil. Boil, uncovered, 20 minutes. Discard fruit. Just before serving, add bourbon. Heat over very low heat just until vapor rises. Remove from heat, ignite with match, and take flaming sauce to table. Spoon over each piece of warm pie.

HEAVENLY PIE WITH GRAHAM SHELL

Serves 8

"Rich, old-fashioned and delicious."

1 pkg. unflavored gelatin
8 Tbs. sugar
⅛ tsp. salt
3 eggs, separated
1 C. milk
⅓ C. molasses
1 Tbs. Maker's Mark
1 C. heavy cream, whipped
⅓ C. slivered almonds

GRAHAM CRACKER PIE SHELL

1¼ C. graham cracker crumbs
¼ tsp. cinnamon
¼ C. sugar
¼ C. butter, melted

- Chill prepared pie shell (see below).
- For filling, mix gelatin, 2 tablespoons sugar and salt in top of double boiler.
- Beat egg yolks and milk together, add to gelatin mixture; also add molasses.
- Cook over boiling water, stirring until mixture is slightly thickened. Remove from heat and stir in bourbon.
- Chill until mixture begins to set. Beat egg whites until stiff. Gradually add 6 tablespoons sugar and beat until very stiff. Fold egg white mixture into gelatin mixture.
- Fold in whipped cream; gently fill pie shell. Chill and decorate with slivered almonds.
- Prepare *Graham Cracker Pie Shell* by mixing crumbs, cinnamon and sugar; then add butter. Press into 9-inch pie pan and chill.

"Coconut is in the crust, filling and topping of this pie. The slight amber color of bourbon in the topping gives that 'just baked' look."

1 envelope unflavored gelatin
1 ⅔ C. milk
½ C. sugar
2 Tbs. cornstarch
¼ tsp. salt
2 eggs, separated
1 Tbs. butter
2 Tbs. Maker's Mark
½ tsp. vanilla
1 C. flaked coconut
½ C. heavy cream , whipped
   and sweetened to taste
1–2 Tbs. Maker's Mark for
   topping

SOUR CREAM COCONUT CRUST

1 C. flour
½ tsp. salt
¼ C. flaked coconut
⅓ C. shortening
2 Tbs. sour cream
2 Tbs. cold water

- For filling, soften gelatin in ⅓ cup milk.

- Combine sugar, cornstarch and salt in medium saucepan; gradually stir in remaining milk. Cook over low heat, stirring constantly, until mixture thickens and boils.

- Remove from heat. Beat egg yolks lightly and stir small amount of hot milk mixture into yolks. Add egg yolk mixture to remaining hot milk mixture. Return to heat and continue to cook, stirring constantly for 2 minutes, then remove from heat.

- Blend into mixture softened gelatin, butter, bourbon and vanilla; cool until lukewarm.

- Beat egg whites until stiff; fold whites and ¾ C. coconut into cooled custard mixture. Pour into pie crust and chill.

- Spread remaining ¼ C. coconut in another pie pan and bake in preheated 350° oven until golden brown; cool. This will toast coconut.

- Just before serving, add bourbon to whipped cream; spread whipped cream over coconut filling and sprinkle with toasted coconut.

- Make *Sour Cream Coconut Crust* by combining flour, salt and coconut. Add shortening; mix at low speed until mixture is crumbly. Add sour cream and water; continue mixing at low speed until dough forms. Shape into ball; roll out on floured surface to circle 1½ inches larger than inverted pie pan. Fit loosely into pie pan, form a rim, flute edge. Prick generously with fork. Bake at 425° for 10–12 minutes.

*"Upside down apple pie looks beautiful and has a taste that is unique.
Pie crust dough can be prepared 1 day ahead."*

¼ C. butter or margarine,
    softened
½ C. pecan halves
½ C. brown sugar
5 large tart apples, peeled,
    cored, and sliced (about
    6 cups)
1 Tbs. orange juice
1 Tbs. Maker's Mark
½ C. granulated sugar
1 Tbs. all-purpose flour
½ tsp. ground cinnamon
½ tsp. ground nutmeg
Dash of salt

EASY PIE CRUST

2 C. all-purpose flour
1 Tbs. sugar
1¼ sticks chilled butter, cut
    into small pieces
¼ C. ice water
1 large egg yolk

SOUR CREAM TOPPING

2 C. sour cream
¼ C. confectioners' sugar
¼ C. Maker's Mark
(Combine ingredients, chill and
    serve over pie.)

- Prepare pie pastry (see below).

- Spread butter evenly on bottom and sides of 9-inch pie plate. Press nuts, rounded side down, into butter on bottom of plate. (Make wagon wheel pattern.) Pat brown sugar evenly over nuts.

- Roll out pastry for bottom crust; place in pie plate over sugar.

- Combine orange juice and bourbon; sprinkle over apples. Mix together sugar, flour, cinnamon, nutmeg, and salt; toss with apples.

- Place apples in pie plate; spread evenly to keep level. Roll out remaining pastry. (If pastry cracks all around the edge as pie crust is being rolled out, turn up cracked edges and press them down, then turn dough over and roll it out again.)

- Cover apples with pie crust; adjust over apples and seal. Prick top of pie with fork. Bake at 400° in preheated oven for 50 minutes.

- Remove from oven; cool 5 minutes. Place serving plate atop pie; invert. Carefully remove pie plate and serve with *Sour Cream Topping*.

- Prepare *Easy Pie Crust* by sifting flour and sugar together; add butter and rub with fingertips until mixture is size of large peas. Combine water and yolk until well blended. Add to flour mixture and toss until dough comes together. Gather dough into ball, wrap in plastic and refrigerate at least 1 hour. When ready to use, roll dough out on floured surface.

"The unusual crust and the quantity of bourbon provide the distinctive flavor to this special treat."

¼ C. cold water
½ C. Maker's Mark
1 Tbs. unflavored gelatin
5 egg yolks
¾ C. granulated sugar
1 C. whipping cream

"BOURBONESE" CRUST

4 Tbs. butter
2 ounces unsweetened chocolate
2 eggs
¼ tsp. salt
1 C. sugar
2 tsp. Maker's Mark
1 C. flour
½ C. pecans, chopped

GARNISH

1½ C. whipped cream
¼ C. confectioners' sugar, sifted
2 tsp. Maker's Mark

- Prepare Bourbonese Crust (see below).

- For filling, combine water and bourbon in top of double boiler, sprinkle gelatin on top, allow to soften.

- Beat egg yolks until thick and lemon colored; add sugar.

- Melt gelatin mixture in double boiler. When dissolved, pour mixture into egg yolks gradually and beat briskly.

- Whip cream, fold into egg mixture and pour into crust. Refrigerate for 4 hours or until set.

- Garnish with whipped cream and chocolate shavings and serve.

- For *Bourbonese Crust*, melt butter and chocolate in double boiler; let cool. Beat eggs and salt until light and foamy.

- Add sugar and bourbon to egg mixture, beat until creamy.

- Stir in chocolate mixture, fold in 1 cup flour and add pecans.

- Press mixture into bottom of springform pan and bake for 25 minutes, then cool.

- Serve with springform pan removed and pie elegantly resting on bottom of pan.

"A southern classic — great ending for a light supper because the pie is so rich."

1 C. sugar (divided into 2 portions)
1 Tbs. cornstarch
2 C. milk, scalded
4 egg yolks, beaten
1 tsp. vanilla
1 C. semi-sweet chocolate pieces
1 envelope unflavored gelatin
½ C. cold water
4 Tbs. Maker's Mark
4 egg whites

GINGER SNAP CRUST

1 C. crisp ginger snaps, crushed
5 Tbs. butter, melted
2 Tbs. sugar

- Prepare pie crust (see below).

- For filling, combine ½ C. sugar and cornstarch; slowly add milk and beaten egg yolks. Stir sugar mixture, then cook and stir in top of double boiler over hot, but not boiling water till custard coats a spoon.

- Remove from heat, add vanilla to 1 cup of custard, add the chocolate pieces and stir till melted. Pour into bottom of crust.

- Next, soften gelatin in ½ cup cold water; add to remaining hot custard. Add bourbon, stir well and chill until slightly thick.

- Beat egg whites, gradually add ½ cup sugar and continue beating until stiff peaks form.

- Fold egg white mixture into custard-gelatin mixture; pile on top of chocolate layer in pie shell. Chill.

- Just before serving, cover pie with bourbon flavored whipped cream, if desired.

- Prepare *Ginger Snap Crust* by pouring melted butter over cookie crumbs and sugar. Stir till crumbs are moistened. Press crumbs firmly over bottom and sides of pie plate. Bake in preheated 350° oven for 10 minutes. When slightly cooled, press crumbs firmly against bottom and sides of pie plate with wooden spoon. Cool completely before filling.

FRUITCAKE SQUARES

Yields 60 squares

"What an easy bar cookie to make for a dessert tray."

⅓ C. butter

1 (12-ounce) box vanilla wafers, finely crushed (3¼ C.)

1 C. pecan halves

¾ C. dates, chopped

¾ C. halved green candied cherries

¾ C. halved red candied cherries

½ C. candied pineapple, chopped

1 (14-ounce) can sweetened condensed milk (1¼ C.)

¼ C. Maker's Mark

- Preheat oven to 350°.

- Melt butter in small saucepan; pour into 10x15-inch baking pan, tilting pan to spread butter evenly. Sprinkle crushed vanilla wafers evenly over butter in pan. Arrange nuts, date and candied fruit evenly over crumb mixture; press down gently.

- Combine sweetened condensed milk and bourbon; pour evenly over top.

- Bake in 350° oven for 20–25 minutes or until set. Cool and cut into squares.

EASY OATMEAL BOURBON COOKIES

Yields 4 dozen

"Occasionally in life we run across ideas that we think are too good to be true. Believe me you'll really enjoy these 'ideal' cookies – they are delicious and so easy to make."

1 C. margarine, softened

½ C. packed brown sugar

1 egg

¼ C. water

1 (2-layer) yellow cake mix

3 Tbs. Maker's Mark

3 C. quick cooking oats

1 C. nuts, chopped

- Preheat oven to 375°.

- Cream margarine and sugar on mixer; add egg, water and ½ pkg. of dry cake mix, blending thoroughly.

- Stir in remaining cake mix, bourbon, oats and nuts.

- Drop dough by teaspoonfuls onto ungreased baking sheet about 2 inches apart. Bake *exactly* 10 minutes. Do not overbake! Cool slightly and remove from baking sheet.

- These cookies will appear "not quite done" when you take them out of the oven, but they will continue cooking on baking sheet.

CHOCOLATE CHIP BITS

Yields 4 dozen

"This cookie is always a favorite with all age groups — I keep an extra batch in the freezer for an emergency dessert."

1 C. butter, softened

¾ C. sugar

¾ C. packed brown sugar

3 Tbs. Maker's Mark

3 C. flour

1 C. chocolate chips

½ C. chopped pecans

- Cream butter, sugars and bourbon on mixer until light and fluffy.

- Add flour; mix in chocolate chips and pecans. (If dough is dry, add 1 tablespoon or more of water.)

- Shape into balls, place on cookie sheet and bake at 350° for 12–13 minutes or until light brown. Cool slightly and remove.

THE HIGHLANDS FRUITCAKE COOKIES
Yields 250 cookies

"These cookies have been served on cookie platters for years in our home at Christmas. Cookies keep for months stored in airtight containers, so start your holiday baking early."

2 sticks butter
1 (16-ounce) box brown sugar
8 eggs (separate yolks and whites)
3½ C. flour (use part to dredge fruit and nuts)
¼ C. Maker's Mark
1 tsp. baking powder
2 lbs. pecans
2 lbs. white raisins
½ lb. candied pineapple
½ lb. candied cherries

- Preheat oven to 275°.
- Cream butter and sugar on electric mixer; add beaten egg yolks.
- Slowly stir in bourbon, flour and baking powder. Add floured nuts and fruit.
- Beat egg whites stiffly and add to fruit mixture.
- Bake cookies on ungreased cookie sheet at 275° for 25–30 minutes.
- This recipe can also be made as a cake. Use tube pan and bake for 2½ hours or use a glass loaf pan and bake for 1½ hours at 275° on upper rack of oven. For cake, don't preheat oven.

SUGAR BABE COOKIES
Yields 5 dozen

"Nothing beats sugar cookies and these are even more special when 'vanilla bean sugar' is sprinkled on each cookie."

1 C. butter
1 C. sugar
2 egg yolks
½ orange rind, grated
½ tsp. mace
1 tsp. vanilla
4 Tbs. Maker's Mark
3¾ all-purpose flour
1 egg white
Granulated sugar for topping

- Preheat oven to 350° and grease cookie sheet.
- Cream butter, add sugar gradually and continue to beat. Add egg yolks, orange rind, mace, vanilla and bourbon. Mix well.
- Slowly add flour until mixture becomes a workable dough. Roll out and cut with cookie cutter. Brush with egg white and sprinkle with granulated sugar or Vanilla Bean Sugar (recipe is in this section).
- Bake at 350° until slightly browned. Watch carefully. Allow to cool.

CHOCOLATE MACAROON PUFFS
Yields 3 dozen

"The chocolate bourbon version of the classic macaroon cookie is always popular on a cookie tray."

2 egg whites
½ C. sugar
¼ tsp. salt
2 tsp. Maker's Mark
1 (6-ounce) pkg. semi-sweet chocolate pieces (melted)
1⅓ C. coconut
½ C. walnuts, chopped

- Preheat oven to 300°.
- Beat egg whites until stiff. Add sugar gradually and continue beating until blended; mix in salt and bourbon. Fold in melted chocolate, coconut and nuts.
- Drop by teaspoonfuls onto baking sheet. Bake in 300° oven for 10–15 minutes. Don't overcook! Remove cookies immediately from cookie sheet to cool.

CRANBERRY COOKIES

"Nice at tea time on a winter afternoon."

1 C. granulated sugar
¾ C. packed brown sugar
½ C. butter, softened
¼ C. orange juice
2 Tbs. Maker's Mark
1 egg
3 C. all-purpose flour
1 tsp. baking powder
½ tsp. salt
¼ tsp. baking soda
2½ C. cranberries, coarsely
   chopped
1 C. nuts, chopped

BROWNED BUTTER GLAZE

⅓ C. butter
2 C. confectioners' sugar
3 Tbs. Maker's Mark
1 tsp. vanilla extract

- Preheat oven to 375°; grease cookie sheet.
- Cream sugars with butter. Stir in orange juice, bourbon and egg. Mix in remaining ingredients.
- Drop by rounded teaspoonfuls about 2 inches apart onto greased cookie sheet. Bake until light brown, 10–15 minutes. Cool; spread with glaze.

- Prepare *Browned Butter Glaze* by heating butter over low heat until golden brown; cool slightly. Stir in confectioners' sugar, bourbon and vanilla. Beat until smooth and of desired consistency. (Add hot water if more liquid is needed.)

FANCY GUMDROP COOKIES

"Instead of gumdrops you can substitute jellied candy orange slices as an ingredient — each is equally good."

½ C. butter
½ C. brown sugar
½ C. white sugar
1 egg
1 C. flour
½ tsp. each of salt and
   baking soda
1 tsp. baking powder
½ C. coconut
½ C. gumdrops, cut up
1 C. quick cooking oats
1 C. corn flakes

- Preheat oven to 350° and grease cookie sheet.
- Cream butter and sugars; add egg and beat until fluffy.
- Sift flour, salt, soda and baking powder, add to creamed mixture and beat until well blended.
- Add coconut, gumdrops, oats and corn flakes. Blend into dough and drop by teaspoonful onto greased baking sheets, about 2 inches apart. Bake at 350° for 15 minutes.
- Add an additional small bit of gumdrop to top of each cookie before baking, if desired.

PARTY BROWNIES

Yields 24 squares

"What a winner for any party!"

1 C. butter

2 squares unsweetened
    chocolate

4 eggs

2 C. sugar

⅛ tsp. salt

3 Tbs. Maker's Mark

1 C. flour, sifted

1 C. nuts, chopped

ICING

¼ C. cocoa

¼ C. butter

2 Tbs. milk

1 C. sugar

2 Tbs. Maker's Mark

1 tsp. vanilla

- Preheat oven to 350°.
- Melt butter and chocolate over hot water in double boiler; set aside to cool. Beat eggs; add sugar, salt and bourbon.
- Add cooled chocolate mixture. Fold in flour and chopped nuts. Pour into greased and floured 9x13-inch pan. Bake at 350° for 45 minutes over pan of hot water.
- For *Icing*, combine all ingredients except bourbon and vanilla; boil 1 minute. Add bourbon and vanilla, beat a few minutes until smooth and pour over brownies.

ABC COOKIES

Yields 4 dozen

"I always call these ABC cookies and that stands for Apricot Bourbon Chews. I've found that people can't believe cookies have apricots in them — and they would rather not know!"

1 C. all-purpose flour

1 tsp. baking soda

1 C. butter

¾ C. packed brown sugar

½ C. sugar

1 egg

1 Tbs. Maker's Mark

2½ C. quick cooking oats

1 C. snipped dried apricots

½ C. finely chopped almonds

2 C. confectioners' sugar

3 Tbs. Maker's Mark

- Preheat oven to 375°.
- Sift together flour and baking soda; set aside.
- Cream butter and sugars; add egg and 1 tablespoon bourbon; beat well. Add flour mixture and beat thoroughly. Stir in oats, apricots and almonds.
- Drop by round teaspoonfuls onto an ungreased cookie sheet. Bake in 375° oven for 8–10 minutes or till done. Cool on cookie sheet for 1 minute, then remove and cool thoroughly.
- Stir together confectioners' sugar and bourbon to make an icing of drizzling consistency and drizzle over cookies.

WHISKY SNAPS

"You can make the snaps days ahead, keeping them dry in a tin. Snaps can be served filled with cream mixture, or not rolled and served as a flat cookie."

¼ C. granulated sugar
¼ C. butter, melted
2 Tbs. maple syrup
½ C. flour
½ tsp. ground ginger
½ tsp. grated orange rind
2 Tbs. Maker's Mark

- Preheat oven to 350° and grease cookie sheet.
- Heat sugar, butter and syrup in saucepan over low heat.
- Mix syrup mixture with flour, ginger, orange rind and 2 tablespoons bourbon.
- Drop 1 teaspoonful at a time on greased or foil-lined (greased) cookie sheet. Leave 5-inch space between snaps for them to spread. (The snaps will harden quickly, so do not try to bake and roll more than 3 snaps at a time. If you have help, you can try 6 snaps each time.)
- When they turn golden and are lacy, approximately 6–8 minutes, remove cookie sheet from oven and quickly roll (with lacy side on the outside) around greased handle of a wooden spoon.

CREAM FILLING

1½ C. heavy cream, whipped
¼ C. confectioners' sugar
2 Tbs. Maker's Mark

- Make *Cream Filling* by combining whipped cream, sugar and bourbon. Fill pastry bag with mixture and pipe cream into each snap.

LEBANON ROCK COOKIES

"This recipe is over 150 years old and has been passed down through several generations in our family. Rock cookies are traditional Christmas fare in Kentucky – every grandmother made lots of them."

6 C. flour
2½ tsp. soda
1 tsp. nutmeg
½ tsp. cloves
1 tsp. cinnamon
2 C. butter
3 C. brown sugar
8 eggs, beaten lightly
6 Tbs. Maker's Mark
2 lbs. seedless raisins
2 lbs. walnuts

- Sift flour with spices and soda.
- Cream butter with sugar; add slightly beaten eggs. Stir in flour (reserving small amount for dredging raisins and nuts). Add bourbon.
- Slowly add raisins and nuts (which have been dredged in flour).
- Allow this cookie mixture to stand overnight in cold temperature before baking. (Grandma put hers in cold pantry.)
- Next day drop mixture by teaspoonful on greased cookie sheet. Bake at 375° for 15 minutes.

IRISH COFFEE COOKIES
Yields 10 dozen

*"These cookies have 'vanilla bean sugar' as a topping. Keep a canister
filled with this sugar in your kitchen at all times."*

1 C. butter, softened
1 C. sugar
2 eggs
1 C. molasses
1 Tbs. vinegar
1 C. hot, very strong coffee
1 Tbs. Maker's Mark
4½ C. sifted flour
½ tsp. ground ginger
2 Tbs. soda
1 tsp. salt

VANILLA BEAN SUGAR

2 vanilla beans
1 lb. granulated sugar

- Preheat oven to 375° and lightly grease cookie sheets.
- Cream butter and sugar; add eggs, molasses, vinegar, coffee and bourbon; blend thoroughly.
- Sift flour, ginger, soda and salt together. Mix liquid with dry ingredients until smooth.
- Drop from teaspoon on lightly greased cookie sheet and bake for 10–12 minutes.
- Remove from oven and sprinkle immediately with vanilla sugar.

- Prepare *Vanilla Bean Sugar* by purchasing 2 vanilla beans at a specialty food shop. Place them in a canister with 1 pound granulated sugar; cover and allow to remain untouched for a week. From time to time replenish sugar; add 1 vanilla bean every 6 months. This sugar gives a much finer flavor than vanilla extract and can be used wherever extract is called for. 1 tablespoon of vanilla sugar equals ¼ teaspoon extract. Decrease amount of sugar in recipe accordingly.

KENTUCKY MINT COOKIES
Yields 8 dozen

"These cookies are very special and disappear quickly."

1 C. butter, softened
½ C. packed brown sugar
1 C. granulated sugar
2 eggs
1 tsp. vanilla
3 C. flour
1 tsp. baking soda
½ teaspoon salt
24 Maker's Mark Mint
  Julep Cremes
Additional granulated sugar
  for topping

- Preheat oven to 375°.
- Cream butter and sugars in large mixing bowl. Add eggs, vanilla and beat well.
- Add flour, baking soda and salt. Mix slowly until dough forms.
- Drop by scant teaspoonfuls 2 inches apart on ungreased baking sheets. Cut each candy in fourths and press ¼ candy on top of each cookie. Cover with another scant teaspoonful of dough. Press and seal edges so candy is completely enclosed.
- Bake in preheated 375° oven for 9–12 minutes. Remove from oven and sprinkle with granulated sugar.

APPLE TREE COOKIES

"Bake these cookies and enjoy the spicy aroma in your kitchen all day."

½ C. margarine
1½ C. brown sugar
2 C. flour
1 tsp. each of soda
   and cinnamon
½ tsp. each of cloves
   and nutmeg
⅛ tsp. salt
1 C. finely chopped
   apples, peeled
1 C. raisins
½ C. nuts, chopped
1 egg
4 Tbs. Maker's Mark

BOURBON GLAZE
1½ C. confectioners' sugar
2½ tsp. Maker's Mark

- Preheat oven to 400° and grease cookie sheets.
- Cream together margarine and brown sugar.
- Sift all dry ingredients together. Add ½ cup of dry ingredients to combined fruit and nuts. Blend in egg and bourbon.
- Add remaining dry ingredients and mix well. Drop by teaspoonfuls on greased baking sheet and bake 10–12 minutes at 400°.

- For *Bourbon Glaze*, mix confectioners' sugar and bourbon. Glaze cookies while hot.

ORANGE TEA CAKES

"The old fashioned jellied orange slices are the prime ingredient for these cookies."

1 C. butter, softened
⅔ C. confectioners' sugar
1 Tbs. Maker's Mark
2¼ C. all-purpose flour
½ C. flaked coconut
1 Tbs. finely shredded
   orange peel
⅛ tsp. salt
16 orange jellied candy slices,
   cut into thirds

GLAZE
1 C. confectioners' sugar
1 Tbs. milk
1 Tbs. Maker's Mark
2-3 drops red food color

- Preheat oven to 400°.
- Combine butter, confectioners' sugar and bourbon; stir in flour, coconut, orange peel and salt. (Refrigerate dough until chilled and firm enough to shape.)
- Shape dough around each small third of orange candy. Bake on ungreased cookie sheet until set, but not brown (8-9 minutes).

- Prepare *Glaze* by mixing all ingredients until smooth and of desired consistency.
- Dip top of cookies into glaze or, for variety, cookies can be rolled in confectioners' sugar while still warm.

CHOCOLATE WHISKY CAKE   Serves 12

"A family favorite of ours and hopefully it will be one of yours!"

4 squares of bitter chocolate
½ C. butter
2 C. sugar
2 eggs, separated
1 tsp. vanilla
2 Tbs. Maker's Mark
2 C. flour, sifted
2 tsp. baking powder
½ tsp. salt
½ C. milk
1 C. pecans, chopped

CHOCOLATE ICING

½ C. butter, softened
¾ C. unsweetened cocoa, sifted
2 Tbs. light corn syrup
1 egg yolk
2 Tbs. Maker's Mark
½ tsp. salt
1 lb. confectioners' sugar, sifted (4½ C.)
3 Tbs. hot milk

- Preheat oven to 350°
- Melt chocolate in double boiler; cool and set aside.
- Cream butter and sugar; add melted chocolate. Slowly add beaten egg yolks, vanilla and bourbon.
- Sift flour 3 times and mix with baking powder and salt. Alternately add flour mixture and milk to chocolate mixture (beginning and ending with flour). Fold in nuts.
- Beat egg whites until stiff and gently fold into mixture.
- Pour into 2 (greased and wax paper-lined) 9-inch cake pans. Bake at 350° for 35 minutes or until done. Frost with chocolate icing.
- Prepare *Chocolate Icing* by combining first 6 ingredients; beat until smooth and satiny. Stir in sugar and hot milk as needed, a small amount at a time, until very smooth and of spreading consistency.

SAUCED FRESH APPLE CAKE   Serves 16

"Everyone loves this cake — and it freezes great — if there's any left."

4 C. fresh apples, peeled, cored, chopped
8 Tbs. Maker's Mark
2 C. flour
2 tsp. each of soda and cinnamon
1 tsp. each of nutmeg and salt
¼ tsp. ground cloves
2 C. sugar
2 eggs
½ C. cooking oil
1 ½ C. pecans, chopped

HOT BUTTERED BOURBON SAUCE

1 C. sugar
½ C. butter
½ C. light cream (half and half)
1 Tbs. Maker's Mark

- Preheat oven to 350°.
- Pour bourbon over apples.
- Sift flour, soda, salt and spices together. Add to apples, tossing to mix.
- Beat together sugar, eggs and oil; add to apple mixture. Add nuts and stir well. Pour into greased and floured 9x13-inch pan. Bake in 350° oven for 1 hour or until done.
- Prepare *Hot Buttered Bourbon Sauce* by combining sugar, butter and cream in saucepan; mix well. Heat over low heat, stirring occasionally, until hot. Stir in bourbon slowly.
- Serve sauce over warm cake.

KENTUCKY HARVEST PEAR CAKE

Serves 12

"What a special way to use all those Kentucky harvest pears. Cake gets better as it ages—it's a terrific cake to keep in freezer for those unexpected guests."

2 C. sugar

3 eggs, beaten

1½ C. cooking oil

3 C. flour

1 tsp. each of soda and salt

1 tsp. vanilla extract

3 C. thinly sliced pears

2 tsp. cinnamon

½ C. walnuts, chopped

WALNUT SAUCE

¼ C. butter

½ C. sugar

⅓ C. packed brown sugar

⅓ C. apple juice

¼ C. Maker's Mark

⅓ C. whipping cream

⅛ tsp. ground nutmeg

½ C. walnuts, chopped

- Preheat oven to 350°; grease tube pan.
- Combine sugar, eggs and oil in bowl; beat well.
- Mix together flour, soda and salt; add 1 cup of flour mixture at a time, mixing well after each addition. Stir in vanilla, pears, cinnamon and nuts.
- Spoon into well-greased tube pan. Bake at 350° for 1 hour or until cake tests done. Cool cake on rack.
- Prepare *Walnut Sauce* by combining first 3 ingredients in heavy skillet. Cook over low heat, stirring constantly, until butter and sugars melt. Continue to cook 3 minutes, without stirring, or until mixture is amber colored. Stir in apple juice and bourbon. Reduce heat and boil until mixture is reduced to ¾ cup. Stir in cream; boil 2–3 minutes or until thickened. Stir in nutmeg and nuts.
- Serve warm sauce over freshly baked cake.

ORANGE CANDY SLICE CAKE

Serves 16

"Memories of the 'orange slice jellied candy days' are brought back with the making of this special cake. It's a perfect way to use those extra candies bought during Christmas."

1 C. butter, softened

1¾ C. sugar

4 eggs

½ tsp. salt

1 tsp. soda

3½ C. self-rising flour

½ C. buttermilk

1½ C. raisins

1 lb. orange candy slices, finely chopped

1½ C. coconut

1½ C. pecans, chopped

ORANGE GLAZE

¾ C. orange juice

¼ C. Maker's Mark

2 C. confectioners' sugar

- Preheat oven to 275°.
- Cream butter and sugar in bowl until light and fluffy. Add eggs, one at a time, beating well after each addition.
- Combine salt, soda and flour mixture, adding alternately with buttermilk; mix well. Stir in raisins, orange slices, coconut and pecans.
- Pour into greased and floured tube pan. Bake at 275° for 2½ hours or until cake tests done.
- Prepare *Orange Glaze* by combining orange juice, bourbon and confectioners' sugar; mix well. Pour over hot cake in pan; cool for 30 minutes or until mixture is absorbed. Invert onto serving plate.

BANANA BOURBON CAKE
Serves 16

"This is a very large, rich cake. It may be frosted with your favorite caramel frosting, if you prefer."

1 C. butter
3 C. sugar
2 C. mashed bananas
4 eggs, beaten
4 C. sifted flour
2 tsp. baking soda
1 C. buttermilk
1 C. pecans, chopped
3 Tbs. Maker's Mark

BANANA FROSTING

½ C. bananas, mashed
2 tsp. lemon juice
⅓ C. butter
2 lbs. confectioners' sugar
1 C. toasted coconut
1 C. walnuts, chopped

- Preheat oven to 350°; grease cake pans.

- Cream butter and sugar together. Add mashed bananas and continue creaming until mixture is smooth. Add beaten eggs and mix slightly.

- Resift flour and soda together. Add to banana mixture alternately with flour and buttermilk (begin and end with flour). Mix in nuts and bourbon.

- Pour batter in 3 (9-inch) layer cake pans. Bake in preheated 350° oven for 45 minutes, or until cake tests done. Cool completely on racks before frosting.

- For *Banana Frosting* sprinkle mashed bananas with lemon juice to prevent darkening. Cream butter, add sugar and bananas, and blend well. Mix in coconut and nuts. Spread between layers and on top and sides of cake.

- *Hint* — Instead of buying buttermilk, I always make my own by warming 1 cup of sweet milk in microwave (1½ minutes on High). Then add 1 tablespoon white vinegar to milk, let set 5 minutes. Milk will sour and is ready to use in any recipe that requires buttermilk.

BOURBON MYSTERY CAKE
Serves 12

"No one will ever guess what's in this cake — but the bourbon definitely adds that special touch."

6 eggs, separated, plus 1
    whole egg
¾ C. sugar
1 C. walnuts, ground finely
⅓ C. butter snack cracker
    crumbs, ground (not saltines)
2 C. heavy cream
4 Tbs. Maker's Mark
2 squares semi-sweet choco-
    late, shaved

- Preheat oven to 350°. Lightly grease 2 (9-inch) cake pans and line with wax paper.

- Beat egg yolks and whole egg with sugar until lemon colored and foamy. Add ground walnuts and cracker crumbs.

- In large bowl beat egg whites until stiff peaks are formed. Gradually fold egg-yolk mixture into egg whites.

- Pour equal amounts of mixture into cake pans and bake in 350° oven for 20 minutes or until surface springs back when gently pressed. Let cool in pans on wire rack.

- Whip cream and slowly add bourbon. Frost cake between the layers, around top and sides. Garnish with chocolate shavings.

RED LANDMARK CAKE WITH BOURBON ICING
Serves 12

"One of the very first cakes I ever made — and it's still one of my favorites. It's perfect for any party."

½ C. butter
1½ C. sugar
2 eggs
2 Tbs. cocoa powder (heaping)
2 ounces red food coloring
  (¼ C.)
2¼ C. cake flour
½ tsp. salt
1 C. buttermilk
1 tsp. vanilla
1 tsp. soda
1 Tbs. white vinegar

BOURBON ICING
_____

1 C. butter, at room
  temperature
1 (8-ounce) pkg. cream cheese,
  softened
2 lbs. confectioners' sugar
5 Tbs. Maker's Mark

- Preheat oven to 350°. Grease and line 2 (8-inch) pans.
- Cream butter with sugar; add eggs. Make paste of cocoa and food coloring; add to creamed mixture.
- Sift flour and salt together; add alternately with buttermilk, then add vanilla.
- Add soda to vinegar; hold over bowl as it foams and blend into cake mixture. Do not beat.
- Bake at 350° in layer pans or tube pan. Cool and frost with Bourbon Icing.
- Prepare *Bourbon Icing* by creaming butter and cream cheese; add confectioners' sugar and bourbon. Mix well until smooth. Spread between layers and on top and sides of cake. Keep cake refrigerated, but remove from refrigerator about 45 minutes before serving.

FIRST SATURDAY IN MAY CAKES
Serves 50

"These cakes are just right for easy entertaining at a large party. Since they are made in advance and aged, there is no last minute preparation and left over cakes can be easily frozen."

¾ C. butter
1¼ C. sugar
8 egg yolks
2½ C. flour, sifted
3 tsp. baking powder
¼ tsp. salt
¾ C. milk
1 tsp. vanilla extract

WHISKY SAUCE
_____

½ C. butter
1 lb. confectioners' sugar, sifted
1 C. Maker's Mark
½ C. pecans, chopped
6 ounces vanilla wafers,
  crushed (½ standard size
  box)

- Preheat oven to 350°. Grease and line with waxed paper (3 square pans).
- Cream butter and sugar until light and fluffy. Add yolks and blend well.
- Sift dry ingredients 3 times; then add to sugar mixture, alternating with milk and vanilla.
- Bake 20 minutes at 350°. After cake cools, cut into small squares.
- Prepare *Whisky Sauce* by creaming butter and confectioners' sugar. Mix well; add bourbon whisky and nuts. Dip squares of cake on all sides in bourbon mix and roll in crumb mix. Store in airtight containers.
- These cakes improve with age. Don't taste for 3 days. Angel food cake squares can be substituted for homemade cake squares.

GINGER-MOLASSES CAKE

Serves 12

"This cake is commonly know as gingerbread. Serve it with a butter-bourbon sauce for an easy, winter treat."

2¾ C. flour, sifted

2½ tsp. ground ginger

1 tsp. each of salt and baking soda

½ tsp. each of cinnamon, nutmeg and ground cloves

1 C. light molasses

½ C. light brown sugar, firmly packed

½ C. butter

¾ C. buttermilk

¼ C. Maker's Mark

2 eggs, beaten

BUTTER-BOURBON SAUCE

1 C. sugar

1 Tbs. cornstarch

¾ C. half-and-half

½ C. butter

2 Tbs. Maker's Mark

- Sift together first 7 ingredients; set aside.
- Combine molasses, sugar and butter in saucepan and bring to a simmer, stirring 2–3 times. Cool to lukewarm.
- Stir cooled molasses mixture and buttermilk into dry ingredients. Add bourbon and eggs, stirring until smooth.
- Pour into well-greased 9x13-inch pan and bake at 350° for 30–35 minutes; or use your most cherished (well-seasoned) black skillet to cook gingerbread in oven. A skillet makes a great pan.
- Prepare *Butter-Bourbon Sauce* by combining sugar, cornstarch, half-and-half and butter in glass bowl; mix well. Microwave on High for 3 minutes; stir. Microwave on High for 4 minutes. Stir in bourbon and serve sauce over warm cake.

SIMPLE POUND CAKE AND RASPBERRIES

Serves 16

"Pound cake is one of the most versatile cakes you can make. It's superb served alone or it can be combined with many other ingredients for a truly elegant dessert."

1½ C. butter

2¾ C. granulated sugar

5 eggs

3¾ C. flour, sifted

⅛ tsp. salt

¼ tsp. baking powder

1 C. milk

1 tsp. vanilla extract

RASPBERRY SAUCE

1 (16-ounce) pkg. frozen red raspberries

1 tsp. cornstarch

1 Tbs. water

¼ C. sugar

½ C. red currant jelly

4 Tbs. Maker's Mark

- Do not preheat oven!
- Cream butter and sugar; add eggs, one at a time.
- Sift flour, salt and baking powder together; add to butter mixture, alternating with milk and vanilla. Beat 1 minute.
- Put cake into cold oven, then turn oven on to 325°; bake for 1½ hours or until knife inserted comes out clean. Cool 10 minutes in pan, then remove to rack to cool.
- Prepare *Raspberry Sauce* by thawing berries; stir berries over low heat until mushy and push through sieve to remove seeds. Mix cornstarch with water, add to strained berries and simmer 5 minutes. Add sugar and currant jelly. Dissolve thoroughly; add bourbon.
- Serve over sliced cake.

"A perfect gift for the person who has everything. This log cake is a fun gift — it's delectable, serves as a Christmas centerpiece, and our friends have come to expect this specialty."

1 C. cake flour, sifted
¼ C. unsweetened cocoa powder
1 tsp. baking powder
¼ tsp. salt
3 large eggs
1 C. granulated sugar
¼ C. water
4 Tbs. Maker's Mark
1 tsp. vanilla extract
Confectioners' sugar

IRISH COFFEE FILLING

1 C. whipping cream, very cold
2 tsp. instant coffee powder
4 tsp. Maker's Mark
½ C. confectioners' sugar, sifted

CHOCOLATE ICING

4 Tbs. butter (½ stick)
2 ounces unsweetened chocolate
2½ C. confectioners' sugar, sifted
¼ C. sour cream
2 Tbs. Maker's Mark
¼ C. pecans, chopped, for garnish

- Preheat oven to 375°. Butter a 10x15-inch jelly-roll pan; line with piece of waxed paper ½-inch smaller than pan and butter paper.

- Sift flour, cocoa, baking powder, and salt together; set aside.

- Beat eggs until thick and creamy. Beat in sugar, 1 tablespoon at a time; continue beating until mixture is very thick. Stir in water, bourbon and vanilla.

- Gently fold in flour mixture until thoroughly combined. Pour batter into prepared pan and spread evenly. Bake at 375° until cake pulls away from sides of pan and springs back when touched lightly in center, 12–15 minutes.

- Trim ¼-inch cake from all sides. Invert cake onto a clean kitchen towel dusted lightly with confectioners' sugar. Peel off waxed paper and, starting with short side, roll up cake in towel like jelly roll. Let cool completely on rack.

- Prepare *Irish Coffee Filling* by beating cream, coffee powder, bourbon and confectioners' sugar in cold mixing bowl until stiff. Carefully unroll cake and spread evenly with filling. Roll up cake again and place on serving plate. Refrigerate while making icing.

- Prepare *Chocolate Icing* by melting butter and chocolate in top of double boiler over simmering water. Cool slightly. Beat confectioners' sugar, sour cream and bourbon together in mixing bowl. Gradually beat in melted chocolate to make a smooth frosting of spreading consistency.

- Finish log by cutting a diagonal slice, 2 inches deep, from one end of cake roll. Place slice about ⅓ of way down roll to resemble a knot of a log. Spread top and sides of cake with chocolate icing. Using lines of a fork, draw lines in icing to resemble bark of a tree. Sprinkle with nuts and sift confectioners' sugar very lightly over top of log. Store in refrigerator until ready to serve.

*"Make cake design by using checkerboard cake pan set — batter should
be stiff for best results. This recipe makes a three-layer cake, but I
always use the extra 3rd layer as a 'before party' dessert dusted with
confectioners' sugar."*

*2½ ounces unsweetened
chocolate (2½ squares)*
4 C. sifted cake flour
4½ tsp. baking powder
1 tsp. salt
2½ C. sugar
1½ C. butter
5 eggs (separated)
2 tsp. vanilla
1¼ C. milk

- Preheat oven to 350° and grease bottom of all cake pans. Line with wax paper circles; grease wax paper. Melt chocolate over low heat; allow to cool.

- Mix flour, baking powder and salt together; set aside.

- Cream butter, slowly adding sugar, beating or mixing all the time. Be sure sugar is well dissolved.

- Beat egg yolks well and add to butter mixture; add vanilla. Stir until well blended. Add flour mixture and milk gradually. Keep mixing.

- Beat egg whites till stiff and fold in mixture.

- Divide batter into 2 equal portions. Add melted chocolate to one portion and mix well.

- Use special checkerboard cake pan set. Put divider in one of the 3 pans. Pour chocolate batter in outer and center rings and vanilla batter in middle ring. Remove divider from pan and put in next pan and repeat.

- Put divider in last pan and pour vanilla batter in outer and center rings. Pour chocolate batter in middle ring and remove divider.

- Bake at 350° for 30–35 minutes. Remove pans from oven; take cakes out of pans and allow to cool. Frost with Barrel Buttercream.

- Prepare *Barrel Buttercream* by melting chocolate chips and unsweetened chocolate in double boiler; cool.

- Beat butter in large bowl of electric mixer until fluffy. Gradually add sugar, beating thoroughly. Add yolks and bourbon. Beat in cooled chocolate.

- Refrigerate until buttercream can be spread easily. Garnish with crushed pecans around sides of cake.

BARREL BUTTERCREAM
1 C. semi-sweet chocolate chips
½ ounce chocolate (½ square)
1½ C. butter
1¼ C. sugar
2 egg yolks
2 Tbs. Maker's Mark

HEAVENLY CAKE WITH BOURBON CREAM FROSTING *Serves 12*

*"This is a superb angel food cake. Add frosting for an elegant dessert —
or just slice and serve freshly baked cake with peaches for simple fare."*

1¼ C. confectioners' sugar
1 C. cake flour
1½ C. egg whites, at room
   temperature (12–14 whites)
1½ tsp. cream of tartar
1 tsp. vanilla extract
¼ tsp. salt
¾ tsp. almond extract
1 C. granulated sugar

EGGNOG FILLING AND
FROSTING
½ C. butter
2 C. confectioners' sugar
2 egg yolks
1 tsp. vanilla
¼ tsp. nutmeg
4 Tbs. Maker's Mark
5 Tbs. light cream
2 C. whipping cream
¼ C. confectioners' sugar, sifted
2 tsp. Maker's Mark

■ Preheat oven to 375°.

■ Stir confectioners' sugar and flour together; set aside.

■ Beat egg whites in large bowl with cream of tartar, vanilla, salt and almond extract until well mixed (on high speed).

■ Continue beating; gradually sprinkle in granulated sugar, 2 tablespoons at a time, until sugar is dissolved and whites stand in stiff peaks. Do not scrape sides of bowl during beating.

■ Fold in flour mixture, about ¼ at a time, just until flour disappears.

■ Pour mixture into ungreased 10-inch tube pan. With knife, cut through batter to break large air bubbles. (Through the years older folk have advised me to thump pan on floor several times to remove air bubbles — and it works.)

■ Bake in 375° oven for 35 minutes, or until cake springs back when lightly touched with finger. Invert cake in pan on Maker's Mark bottle; cool for 2 hours. With knife, loosen cake from pan and cut into 4 horizontal layers with serrated knife.

■ Prepare *Eggnog Filling and Frosting* by creaming butter with sifted sugar till fluffy. Blend in 1 egg yolk at a time. Stir in vanilla, nutmeg, bourbon and light cream. Spread on cake layers and reassemble cake. Whip heavy cream, gradually add confectioners' sugar and 2 tsp. bourbon, mixing well. Frost cake and refrigerate at least 6 hours before serving.

"After baking, wrap cake in cloth which has been dampened in Maker's Mark and place in tin container. Add apple slices, cover container, and let set until cake has aged 3-4 weeks or longer. Cake will keep indefinitely when stored in cool place, but don't refrigerate."

1½ C. butter, softened
2 C. granulated sugar
2¼ C. packed light brown sugar
6 eggs
5½ C. flour
¼ tsp. salt
1 tsp. ground nutmeg
2 C. Maker's Mark
3¾ C. pecans, coarsely chopped

- Preheat oven to 300°. Heavily grease a 10-inch tube pan. Flour lightly and shake out excess; set aside.

- Combine granulated sugar and brown sugar together. In large bowl, cream butter until smooth; add ½ sugar mixture; mix well.

- Beat eggs in another mixing bowl until light and fluffy. Slowly beat in remaining sugar mixture. Continue beating until mixture is smooth and creamy. Add to the butter mixture and stir until thoroughly combined.

- Sift flour, salt and nutmeg together. Add flour mixture and bourbon alternately to batter, beginning and ending with flour; mix thoroughly. Stir in pecan pieces.

- Place batter in tube pan and bake for 1½–1¾ hours or until cake begins to shrink from sides of pan.

- Remove from oven and cool in pan for 15 minutes. Turn out onto rack and cool completely.

- This recipe will make several gift-size pecan cakes when baked in standard round one-pound coffee cans that have been emptied and greased. After baking, decorate cans and use as gift containers for cakes.

SPECIAL TOUCH FRUITCAKE   *Yields 14 pounds*

*"Keep fruitcake fresh by storing in very cool area of your house (not the
refrigerator). Do not chop fruits or nuts, except cut cherries into halves.
Best when served in thin slices, so cut with a very sharp knife."*

1 lb. cherries, candied
24 ounces mixed fruit, candied
1 lb. box raisins
8 ounces pineapple, candied
2 C. Maker's Mark
6 C. flour
1 tsp. each of salt and nutmeg
2 tsp. cinnamon
3 tsp. baking powder
2 C. margarine
3 C. sugar
12 eggs
8 ounces strawberry jam
1½ lbs. pecans
1½ lbs. walnuts

MAKER'S SYRUP
2 C. water
1½ C. sugar
1 C. Maker's Mark

- Preheat oven to 275°. Line pans with brown paper and grease.

- Combine all fruits and soak overnight in bourbon. (Cut cherries into halves.) Reserve leftover bourbon from fruit and add later. Dredge fruit in flour (small amount) before adding to batter. Combine dry ingredients and set aside.

- Cream margarine and sugar until light and fluffy. Beat in eggs, one at a time. Stir in jam and reserved bourbon; thoroughly mix.

- Lightly fold flour and spice mixture into creamed batter.

- Combine batter and fruit in large bowl; add pecans and walnuts. Pour into 2 large tube pans or 5 small loaf pans. (Be sure pans are well-greased and floured.)

- Bake in 275° oven. Loaf pans will take 1½–2 hours to cook; tube pans will take 2–3 hours. (Cakes are done when tester comes out clean.)

- Prepare *Maker's Syrup* by boiling water and sugar until sugar is dissolved. Remove from heat and pour in bourbon. Pour over hot cakes from oven. Leave cakes in pans till thoroughly cooled.

- Decorate tops of cakes with additional candied fruit and slice very thinly when serving.

- After several months, freeze fruitcake to preserve freshness.

"Iron skillet cooking is popular in Kentucky and the South. This cake is just one more reason to have a black iron skillet in your kitchen."

1 stick butter

1 C. brown sugar, firmly
   packed

8 slices unsweetened pineapple

4 eggs, separated

1 Tbs. butter, melted

1 tsp. vanilla extract

½ tsp. nutmeg

⅛ tsp. salt

1 C. sugar, sifted

1 C. cake flour

1 tsp. baking powder

SAUCE

1½ C. pineapple juice

¼ C. Maker's Mark

■ Preheat oven to 350°.

■ Melt stick of butter in large iron skillet; stir in brown sugar and cook over low heat until sugar is completely dissolved. Arrange pineapple slices in melted sugar by symmetrical pattern. (This will be the top of the finished cake.)

■ Beat egg yolks in mixing bowl until thick; add 1 tablespoon melted butter, vanilla and nutmeg.

■ Beat egg whites in another mixing bowl, adding salt. When whites begin to hold shape, slowly add the sifted sugar. Fold stiffly beaten egg whites into yolk mixture.

■ Sift flour and baking powder together; fold into batter slowly. Spoon batter over pineapple-sugar layer, smoothing top.

■ Bake at 350° for 25–30 minutes or until cake puffs and turns golden. Remove from oven and let cool 15 minutes. If serving immediately, turn upside down on serving plate. If cake has been baked in advance, leave in skillet and when ready to serve, warm in 325° oven for 10 minutes, then remove to serving plate.

■ For *Sauce*, boil pineapple juice until it reduces to 1 cup. (This can be done in advance.) Just before serving, reheat juice, adding bourbon. Boil for 1 minute. Serve sauce over warm cake.

"No one will recognize that zucchini is the star ingredient in this special treat — but everyone will appreciate this moist, dense cake."

9 Tbs. butter, softened
2 C. sugar
3 (1-ounce) squares
   unsweetened chocolate,
   melted and cooled
3 eggs
½ C. milk
2 tsp. vanilla extract
2 tsp. grated orange rind
2 C. unpeeled zucchini,
   coarsely grated
2½ C. all-purpose flour
2½ tsp. baking powder
1½ tsp. baking soda
½ tsp. salt
1 tsp. ground cinnamon

BOURBON GLAZE
_____
4 Tbs. butter
2 Tbs. brown sugar
¼ C. granulated sugar
3 Tbs. Maker's Mark
¼ C. apple cider
2 Tbs. orange juice
2 Tbs. heavy cream

■ Preheat oven to 350°; grease and flour a 10-inch Bundt pan.

■ Cream butter; gradually add sugar, beating until light and fluffy. Beat in chocolate. Add eggs, one at a time, beating well after each addition.

■ Beat in milk, vanilla, orange rind and zucchini.

■ Combine flour, baking powder, soda, salt and cinnamon; add to creamed mixture, mixing well.

■ Pour batter into Bundt pan; bake at 350° for 1 hour or until wooden pick inserted in center comes out clean. Cool in pan 10–15 minutes; remove from pan and cool on rack.

■ Prepare *Bourbon Glaze* by melting butter in small pan over medium heat. Stir in remaining ingredients briskly to mix. Bring to boil, stirring constantly. Reduce heat to low and simmer 6 minutes. Cool 5 minutes; blend again and pour or brush on slightly cooled cake.

SLEEPY CANDIES

Yields 30 pieces

"The Bourbon Chocolate Candies can stand alone (they are delicious) or be combined with other ingredients for fantastic results."

12 Bourbon Creme Chocolate
  Candies
2 egg whites, stiffly beaten
¾ C. sugar

- Preheat oven to 350°.
- Chop candies finely in food processor or blender. (Candies should be cold when chopped.)
- Beat egg whites to stiff peaks. Fold sugar and candies into egg whites.
- Drop by teaspoonfuls onto foil-lined cookie sheet. Place in preheated 350° oven and turn oven off immediately. Leave in oven overnight!
- The Bourbon Chocolate Candies are available by mail from Erhler's Candies and Maker's Mark Gift Gallery. Ordering information is available in back of this book.

STRAWBERRY - BOURBON CREME DELIGHTS

Serves 12

"This is not a candy — but so elegant when served with bourbon candies on a pewter tray."

1 pt. fresh strawberries,
  with stems
4 ounces cream cheese,
  softened
3 Tbs. confectioners' sugar
2 tsp. Maker's Mark

- Rinse strawberries, gently pat dry.
- In small bowl, combine cream cheese, sugar and bourbon; blend well.
- Dip berries into cream cheese mixture, coating bottom half of berry.
- Arrange on serving tray; cover and refrigerate until serving. (One pint of strawberries contains approximately 25–35 medium-sized strawberries.)

TOO EASY FUDGE

Yields 48 pieces

"A super simple recipe that delivers a premium fudge."

4½ C. granulated sugar
1 (13-ounce) can evaporated
  milk
18 ounces semi-sweet chocolate
  pieces
½ lb. butter
1 Tbs. Maker's Mark
2 C. pecans, chopped

- Combine sugar and milk in saucepan. Bring to boil; boil over medium heat for exactly 6 minutes, stirring constantly.
- Remove from heat, adding remaining ingredients; mix well.
- Spread evenly in greased 9x13-inch dish and allow to set up in cool place for 6 hours before cutting.

PERFECT DIVINITY WITH BOURBON PECANS   *Yields 36 pieces*

"Simply divine candy."

3 egg whites, stiffly beaten
4 C. granulated sugar
1 C. light corn syrup
¾ C. water
1 tsp. vanilla

- Beat egg whites to stiff peaks and leave in mixing bowl.

- Combine sugar, corn syrup and water in saucepan over low heat. Stir until sugar is dissolved.

- Cook *without* stirring until it reaches 225°, or when 1 teaspoonful, dropped from spoon into cold water, forms hard ball.

- Remove from heat and pour, beating constantly, in a fine stream into egg whites. Continue beating until mixture holds its shape and loses its gloss. Add vanilla and stir.

- Drop quickly from spoon onto waxed paper in individual peaks; top each piece with a bourbon pecan.

BOURBON PECANS

2 C. whole pecans
6 Tbs. Maker's Mark

- For *Bourbon Pecans*, heat oven to 300° F. Grease 10x15-inch jelly roll pan with oil. In small bowl combine pecans and bourbon; arrange in single layer on pan. Bake for 20–25 minutes or until glazed and lightly browned, stirring often. Cool.

BOURBON STUFFED DATES   *Yields 24 pieces*

"This candy is an old favorite from years ago and is very special served around a pork roast — don't limit your combinations of food."

1 lb. pitted dates
1 C. Maker's Mark
1 C. pecan halves
½ C. granulated sugar

- Soak dates in bourbon, turning occasionally, until most of bourbon is absorbed, about 24 hours.

- Place pecan half in each date; press to close.

- Roll in sugar and store in airtight container in refrigerator.

KENTUCKY CREAM CANDY   *Yields 60 pieces*

"Candy this good shouldn't be so easy."

1 (8-ounce) pkg. cream cheese, softened
¼ tsp. salt
1 Tbs. Maker's Mark
6 C. confectioners' sugar (sifted)
1 C. black walnuts, finely chopped

- Beat cream cheese, salt and bourbon with electric mixer till smooth.

- Add 2 cups confectioners' sugar, a little at a time, beating on high speed.

- Add remaining sugar and mix well. Cover and chill in refrigerator till firm.

- Shape into small balls and roll in walnuts. Store in airtight container and refrigerate.

"THE HIGHLANDS" BOURBON BALLS — *Yields 24 balls*

"Our favorite candy, served especially during the holidays. Make this candy several days before serving so flavors can age."

1 C. pecans
4 Tbs. Maker's Mark
1 stick butter or margarine
1 (16-ounce) box powdered sugar
½ box semi-sweet chocolate squares
½ rectangle of paraffin (for dipping candies)

- Combine pecans and bourbon; wait at least 3 hours for pecans to absorb bourbon flavor.
- Cream butter and powdered sugar with mixer, adding bourbon and pecan mixture.
- Roll mixture into small balls and chill in refrigerator for 1½ hours.
- Melt chocolate in double boiler, adding shaved paraffin. Heat until thoroughly melted.
- Dip balls into chocolate and put on waxed paper to dry. (Use a fork or long skewer when dipping balls.)

BOURBON FUDGE — *Yields 64 pieces*

"The microwave oven combines with 'that special touch' for marvelous fudge."

1 (12-ounce) pkg. semi-sweet chocolate chips
1 (14-ounce) can sweetened condensed milk
¼ C. Maker's Mark
½ tsp. orange extract
1 (¾-ounce) pkg. slivered almonds

- Combine chocolate chips and milk in large bowl and cover loosely. Cook in microwave for 3 minutes on High.
- Remove from microwave and stir until smooth. Add bourbon and orange extract; mix well.
- Grease an 8-inch square pan and sprinkle bottom of pan with almonds. Pour mixture in pan; let stand until firm or chill in refrigerator.

MOCHA MARK BALLS — *Yields 4 dozen balls*

"Hickory nuts add a special Kentucky touch to any candies, but you can substitute pecans or walnuts, if they are not available."

3 Tbs. coffee granules
⅓ C. Maker's Mark
2 C. vanilla wafer crumbs
1 C. confectioners' sugar
1 C. hickory nuts, chopped
3 Tbs. light corn syrup
2 Tbs. baking cocoa
¼ C. confectioners' sugar for coating

- Dissolve coffee granules in bourbon.
- Combine all ingredients except the confectioners' sugar that will be used for coating.
- Shape by rounded teaspoonfuls into balls. Roll in the additional confectioners' sugar.

NUTTY FUDGE

Yields 24 pieces

"The combination of pecans and walnuts adds a special flavor to this candy. I use this blending of nuts in many dishes because I like it — not because I can't make up my mind which nuts to use."

3 C. granulated sugar
¼ C. light corn syrup
3 Tbs. butter
½ tsp. salt
1 C. evaporated milk
2 Tbs. Maker's Mark
½ C. water
2 tsp. vanilla extract
½ C. walnuts, chopped
½ C. pecans, chopped

- Combine first 7 ingredients in medium-sized heavy saucepan. Heat, stirring constantly, to boiling; then cook rapidly, stirring several times, to 238° on a candy thermometer (a teaspoon of syrup should form a soft ball when dropped in cold water).
- Remove from heat; add vanilla, but do not stir. Cool mixture in pan to 110°, beat 3 minutes until mixture starts to thicken and loses gloss; add nuts.
- Spread in buttered 8-inch square dish. Let stand until set; cut into pieces and wait 24 hours before serving.

WHISKY BALLS

Yields 5 dozen balls

"What an unusual combination of ingredients — but very delicious."

1 (6-ounce) pkg. semi-sweet chocolate chips
1 (7-ounce) jar marshmallow creme
2 Tbs. Maker's Mark (or more, if desired)
3 C. crisp rice cereal
½ C. coconut, shredded
¾ C. walnuts, chopped

- Melt chocolate in top of double boiler; allow to cool, but not set.
- Combine melted chocolate, marshmallow creme, and bourbon; stir well. Add cereal, coconut and walnuts; stir gently to blend.
- Shape into 1-inch balls; chill until firm. Whisky balls may be rolled in additional ground walnuts or coconut, if desired.

KENTUCKY TRUFFLES

Yields 40 pieces

"The Kentucky version of the traditional English candy."

⅓ C. butter
½ C. cocoa
2¾ C. powdered sugar
½ C. whipping cream
3 Tbs. Maker's Mark
40 walnuts

CANDY COATING
2 Tbs. cocoa
3 Tbs. powdered sugar

- Melt butter, stir in cocoa and beat. Combine this cocoa mixture with powdered sugar in large mixing bowl, gradually adding cream and bourbon. Mix well.
- Chill mixture until firm and shape small amount of mixture around each walnut forming 1-inch balls.
- Roll in powdered sugar or mixture of powdered sugar and cocoa.
- Cover and chill until firm or freeze up to six weeks. (Reroll in more coating before serving.)

"STILL HOUSE" PRALINES

Yields 12 pieces

"These pralines are so scrumptious, you'll need to make several batches because they disappear fast!"

1 C. granulated sugar
2 C. light brown sugar
¼ C. light corn syrup
⅛ tsp. salt
1¼ C. milk
1 Tbs. Maker's Mark
1 tsp. almond extract
1½ C. pecan halves

- Combine first 6 ingredients in saucepan. Bring to boil, cook without stirring until mixture registers 236° on candy thermometer (½ tsp. of mixture dropped in cold water should form a soft ball).
- Add almond extract and pecans to mixture; beat with spoon until mixture begins to thicken and loses gloss.
- Drop from tablespoon onto waxed paper and spread to form patties about 4 inches in diameter.
- Let stand till firm.

FESTIVE FRUIT CANDY

Yields 36 balls

"This is a no-cook candy that is colorful to serve and full of healthful ingredients."

¾ C. pitted dried prunes
¾ C. whole dates
½ C. dried apricots
½ C. whole almonds
¼ C. raisins
2 Tbs. Maker's Mark
2 tsp. molasses
1¼ C. coconut

- Grind together dried prunes, dates, apricots, almonds and raisins. (Use a coarse blade on a food processor or grinder.) Put in mixing bowl, add bourbon and molasses and stir till well combined.
- Shape mixture into 1-inch balls; roll in coconut and store tightly covered in refrigerator.

DATE BALLS WITH SPIRIT

Yields 50–60 balls

"Date balls can be served as either a candy or a cookie. They are a special addition to any candy assortment tray."

1 C. butter
1½ C. granulated sugar
2 C. dates, chopped
2½ Tbs. Maker's Mark
⅛ tsp. salt
2 eggs, well beaten
4½ C. crispy rice cereal
½ C. pecans
½ C. confectioners' sugar for coating

- Melt butter and sugar; add dates and cook till mixture pulls away from sides of pan (similar to cream puffs).
- Slowly add bourbon, salt and eggs.
- Remove from heat; add cereal and pecans. Let cool until you can shape into balls with hands.
- Roll in powdered sugar or coconut.

THE MAKER'S CREAM BARS
Yields 3 pounds

"This candy is worth the trouble — a real treat for anyone!"

½ C. butter
¼ C. white sugar
¼ C. cocoa
1 egg, beaten
1 Tbs. Maker's Mark
2 C. graham crackers, finely
   ground

BOURBON CREAM

½ C. butter
1 (16-ounce) box confectioners'
   sugar
¼ C. Maker's Mark
½ C. pecans, finely chopped

CHOCOLATE TOPPING

1 (6-ounce) pkg. semi-sweet
   chocolate chips
3 Tbs. butter

- Line a 9-inch square pan with waxed paper; leave an overhang.

- Melt butter in medium saucepan over very low heat. Stir in sugar and cocoa; cook until thoroughly dissolved. Remove from heat and cool slightly, about 5 minutes.

- Slowly stir ¼ C. of cooled mixture into beaten egg; return egg mixture back to remaining mixture in saucepan.

- Heat again over low heat, stirring in bourbon gradually. Add ground graham crackers and mix well.

- Press mixture into lined pan and chill.

- For *Bourbon Cream*, cream butter and sugar; beat in bourbon slowly until mixture is consistency of very thick cream. Stir in nuts and spread immediately over chocolate base.

- Make *Chocolate Topping* by melting chocolate with butter over low heat. Swirl over chilled Bourbon Cream; chill until set or overnight.

DERBY BOURBON BALLS
Yields 30 balls

"I just couldn't resist including a very unusual bourbon ball recipe. These candies are especially delightful when served during the Derby festivities in May."

24 lemon wafers
1 C. pecans, chopped finely
1 C. superfine granulated
   sugar
2 Tbs. cocoa
⅔ C. Maker's Mark
2 Tbs. honey
½ C. confectioners' sugar
1 tsp. cinnamon

- Crush lemon wafers and place crumbs in bowl with pecans, granulated sugar, cocoa, bourbon and honey; mix together thoroughly.

- Drop from a teaspoon onto baking sheet and chill.

- After chilling, roll on waxed paper into marble-size balls.

- Sift together confectioners' sugar and cinnamon; roll balls in mixture and let stand until sugar is partially absorbed. Then roll in sugar mixture again.

- Store between layers of waxed paper in airtight container.

- *Hint*— You can make superfine sugar in your kitchen by processing granulated sugar in a food processor for 2–3 minutes or whatever time is needed to achieve superfine sugar consistency.

For every great idea Bill Samuels Sr. had for making whisky, his wife, Margie, had an equally good idea for packaging it.

Margie wanted the label to say premium even before you tasted the bourbon. Since fine cognacs are sealed, she came up with the idea of dipping and sealing the bottle in red wax.

This process gives each bottle its own personality and adds a special loving touch… one of three hugs every bottle gets as it moves through the bottling and packing process.

For the first few years, Margie kept the wax hot in her deep fat fryer. Today, the fryer is long gone, but each bottle is still hand-dipped, making each one as unique and individual as a snowflake.

The seal is also our distinctive trademark brought to the bottle by Margie. A collector of pewter, she knew the maker of pewter put his mark on each piece. So she created the "S" representing the long-standing Samuels name, a "IV" to represent four generations of Samuels distillers and a star for Star Hill Farms. (It was later discovered through research that it should be "VI".) Incidentally, that's how "Maker's Mark" got its name.

Opposite side photo: (left to right)
Strawberry-Bourbon Trifle, Samuels'
Parfait, Angel Orange Delight, Star Hill Nut
Bourbon Buns, Bourbon and Lime Sauced
Melon Balls, Loretto Coffee

WHISKY ORANGE SLICES

Yields 4 cups

"Another great gift for the person who loves to add 'that special touch' to entertaining."

4 seedless oranges
2½ C. sugar
1 C. water
1 C. light corn syrup
1 Tbs. lemon juice
⅓ C. Maker's Mark

■ Wash and cut orange, rind and all, into ½-inch thick slices; cut each slice in half. Add orange slices to a glass jar and arrange in overlapping layers.

■ Combine sugar, water, corn syrup and lemon juice. Stir Maker's Mark into syrup mixture and spoon over orange slices, covering them completely. Seal jar and store in cool place.

■ Serve over vanilla ice cream, plain cake slices, or use as garnish in cocktails such as old-fashioneds and sours.

MAKER'S PARADISE CREAM

Yields 1 quart

"A superlative cream that makes a perfect hostess gift. It's the star ingredient in Maker's Paradise Cake — another special remembrance for a friend."

1 (14-ounce) can sweetened
   condensed milk
1 C. heavy cream
3 eggs, beaten slightly
2 Tbs. chocolate syrup
1 tsp. vanilla extract
1 C. Maker's Mark

■ Combine condensed milk, cream, eggs, chocolate syrup and vanilla extract. Mix thoroughly and whisk in bourbon.

■ Store mixture in covered quart jar and refrigerate overnight. Mixture will keep at least 1 week in refrigerator.

CHOCOLATE-DIPPED STRAWBERRIES

Yields 24

"This pretty dessert couldn't be simpler."

6 ounces semi-sweet chocolate
2 Tbs. butter
2 tsp. Maker's Mark
24 large strawberries (washed,
   but not capped)

■ Combine chocolate, butter and bourbon over moderate heat. Melt mixture, stirring frequently, until smooth — about 5 minutes; remove from heat.

■ Cover plate with waxed paper. Holding on to stem, dip strawberry halfway into chocolate and place on prepared platter. Repeat with remaining berries. Refrigerate about 10 minutes or until set, but don't store in refrigerator.

■ Store dipped berries in cool place for up to 1 day.

STAR HILL NUT BOURBON BUNS

Yields 24 rolls

"These sticky yeast rolls are good enough for dessert anytime."

1 C. milk, scalded
½ C. butter
⅓ C. sugar
1½ tsp. salt
1 pkg. dry yeast
¼ C. warm water
3 eggs
5½ C. flour, sifted

NUT BOURBON FILLING

½ C. butter, softened
1 C. packed light brown sugar
2 tsp. cinnamon
¾ C. pecans, chopped
¾ C. dark corn syrup
3 Tbs. Maker's Mark

- Combine first 4 ingredients and stir until butter melts and sugar dissolves. Cool to lukewarm.
- Soften yeast in warm water and add to liquids. Stir in eggs and enough flour to make a soft, moderately stiff dough. Place on lightly floured board and knead until smooth and elastic.
- Place in greased bowl, turning once to coat thoroughly. Cover and let rise in warm place until double in size, about 1½–2 hours.
- Turn dough onto lightly floured board, and divide in half. Roll out each half (¼-inch thick) into a 10x18-inch rectangle.
- Spread each rectangle with softened butter. Combine sugar and cinnamon and sprinkle half over each rectangle; scatter nuts over dough. Mix together syrup and bourbon thoroughly but don't put on dough.
- Butter 2 (9-inch) pans and drizzle ½ syrup mixture over surface of each pan.
- Roll each portion of dough in jelly-roll fashion; starting on long side, cut each roll into 12 slices and place flat on pans. Cover and let rise until double in size (about 45–60 minutes.)
- Bake at 350° for 30 minutes, or until done. Turn out of pans onto baking sheet immediately. Let all syrup drip out of pans onto rolls.

LAST MINUTE CHOCOLATE MOUSSE

Serves 4

"This recipe can easily be doubled for a dinner party. It takes only 5 minutes to make and 1 hour to chill, but the raves of praise are unending!"

4 squares semi-sweet chocolate
5 Tbs. orange juice
4 eggs, separated
2 Tbs. Maker's Mark

- Combine chocolate and orange juice in double boiler; over low heat melt mixture, stirring occasionally to prevent burning. Cool slightly.
- Beat egg whites until they form soft peaks. In separate bowl, stir melted chocolate into egg yolks; add bourbon slowly. Fold this into beaten egg whites, combining thoroughly.
- Spoon into serving dishes and chill for 1 hour before serving.

BLUEGRASS MERINGUES AND PEACHES　　　Serves 6

"Fill meringues with ice cream or fresh fruit and top with a flavored sauce — you'll have a light dessert that is always special. Meringues have been served in our family for several generations — they mean company's coming to our house."

2 egg whites, at room
　　temperature
⅛ tsp. salt
⅔ C. sugar
1 tsp. vanilla extract
1 C. walnuts, coarsely chopped

- Preheat oven to 350°.
- Beat egg whites with salt until foamy.
- Gradually add sugar (1 tablespoon at a time), beat until stiff. By hand, fold in vanilla and nuts.
- Place brown or white paper on baking sheet and spoon mixture by tablespoonfuls onto paper. Hollow out center of each mound with back of spoon; or put through a pastry tube with large tip.
- Place baking sheet in 350° oven and immediately cut off heat. Allow to remain in oven overnight. (Do not open oven door until morning.)
- Meringues can be made in varying sizes. I usually make 4-inch diameter meringues to serve, or combine 3 small meringues on dessert dish (for 1 serving) and top with *Bluegrass Peaches*. (Keep meringues in airtight container and they will keep fresh for a month.)

BLUEGRASS PEACHES

6 Tbs. brown sugar
6 Tbs. Maker's Mark
6 peach halves (canned)
6 tsp. butter

- Prepare *Bluegrass Peaches* by combining brown sugar and bourbon until sugar dissolves. Pour sauce over peach halves; add 1 teaspoon of butter to each half. Bake in 325° oven until sauce is hot. Serve over meringues filled with ice cream.

LORETTO COFFEE　　　Serves 6

"Serve in clear glass coffee mugs and it will look as good as it tastes."

6 C. strong coffee
12 tsp. brown sugar
12 Tbs. Maker's Mark
1 C. heavy cream, whipped
　　stiffly
Cinnamon, for garnish

- Perk coffee about 30 minutes before preparing after dinner drink; whip cream just before serving.
- Measure 2 teaspoons brown sugar (or less, if preferred) and 2 tablespoons bourbon into each coffee cup. Add hot coffee, leaving about 1 inch of space at top of cup; stir to dissolve sugar.
- Carefully spoon some whipped cream on top of coffee. Let cream slide down back of spoon and it will float on hot coffee rather than mixing with it. (Cover surface of coffee liberally with whipped cream; sprinkle cinnamon on top of cream.)

ICE CREAM — YOUR WAY

"One of my family's favorite desserts — keep in the freezer for serving after any meal. I've included 3 'special' sauces that can be served over ice cream — choose your favorite."

Any flavor ice cream for eight
1 C. pecans, chopped

BOURBON FUDGE SAUCE

2 Tbs. butter
1 C. granulated sugar
3 Tbs. cocoa
¼ C. boiling water
2 Tbs. light corn syrup
¼ tsp. salt
2 Tbs. Maker's Mark

HOT STRAWBERRY SAUCE

1 qt. fresh strawberries
1 C. sugar, or to taste
4 Tbs. Maker's Mark

AGED BUTTERSCOTCH SAUCE

3 C. packed brown sugar
1 C. light corn syrup
½ C. margarine
½ C. whipping cream
1 Tbs. Maker's Mark

- Using scoop, make balls of ice cream about size of tennis balls. Roll in chopped pecans; place on wax paper-lined tray in freezer to harden. Transfer to covered container for extended storage.

- Serve by topping with any 3 of my favorite sauces.

- Prepare *Bourbon Fudge Sauce* by melting butter in saucepan. Blend in sugar and cocoa well; add boiling water slowly to butter and stir well. Add corn syrup and bring mixture to a boil; boil 5 minutes. Cool, add salt and bourbon.

- Prepare *Hot Strawberry Sauce* by hulling fresh berries and cutting in half. Put berries in saucepan with sugar. Simmer until soft but not mushy. Remove from heat and add bourbon. Serve warm over ice cream. (Don't make sauce in advance, prepare just before serving).

- Prepare *Aged Butterscotch Sauce* by heating first 3 ingredients to boiling over medium heat, stirring constantly. Remove from heat; stir in whipping cream and bourbon. Serve warm or cool; or pour into jars and cover tightly for use later. Refrigerate no longer than 3 months.

FAVORITE MILK PUNCH

"Keep punch ingredients available for drop-in guests — it's a quick drink for impromptu entertaining."

1½ C. milk
1½ C. half-and-half
½ C. white crème de cacao
½ C. Maker's Mark
2 Tbs. confectioners' sugar
2 egg whites
¼ tsp. ground cinnamon

- Combine all ingredients, except cinnamon, in container of electric blender; blend until frothy.

- Serve over cracked ice and sprinkle with cinnamon.

STRAWBERRY-BOURBON TRIFLE

Serves 16

"This easy Scottish dessert combines jam-covered, spirit-soaked pound cake with a rich custard sauce and whipped cream. Macaroons, ladyfingers, sponge or angel food cake may be substituted for the pound cake — even leftover cakes or cookies can be used to create infinite variations."

1 large pound cake,
   cut into strips
1 C. strawberry jam
⅔ C. Maker's Mark
1 C. whole strawberries, for
   garnish

CUSTARD SAUCE

4 Tbs. flour
1 C. sugar
¼ tsp. salt
4 eggs
4 C. milk
2 tsp. vanilla

PERFECT WHIPPED CREAM

1 tsp. unflavored gelatin
2 Tbs. cold water
2 C. whipping cream

- Line crystal dish or large trifle stand with half of cake strips. Spread cake generously with jam and sprinkle with ⅓ cup bourbon. Set aside.

- Make *Custard Sauce* by mixing flour, sugar and salt. Beat eggs lightly and blend with sugar. Scald milk and gradually add to sugar mixture. Cook over hot water, stirring constantly, until sauce thickens and coats a wooden spoon. Cool, add vanilla and chill.

- Pour ½ custard mixture over cake in bowl. Add remaining cake, jam, bourbon and custard in layers as before. Top with whipped cream and strawberries.

- Prepare *Perfect Whipped Cream* by sprinkling gelatin over cold water in saucepan. Place over hot water and stir until gelatin is dissolved. Add whipping cream and chill. Whip mixture until it holds soft peaks, then dollop over finished trifle. (This is a recipe for whipped cream that will keep in refrigerator for several days.)

- This recipe makes a very large dessert which will keep in refrigerator for 2–3 days.

STRAWBERRIES AND CREAM

Serves 8

"This is a fabulous dessert — and there's always room for it after any meal."

1 qt. strawberries
½ C. confectioners' sugar
8 Tbs. Maker's Mark
1 C. whipping cream
1 pt. vanilla ice cream, softened

- Mix washed strawberries with confectioners' sugar and 3 Tbs. bourbon; chill.

- Whip cream and fold into ice cream. Gently add 5 Tbs. bourbon.

- Blend ice cream mixture and strawberry mixture together quickly and serve in stemmed glasses. (Have both mixtures ready and chilled, but do not blend until ready to serve.)

AWARD WINNING CHEESECAKE

Serves 16

"Cheesecake is one of the most popular desserts today. Make this one at least 1 day before serving to enhance flavor. To keep top from cracking, don't open oven door during baking."

3 (8-ounces each) pkgs. cream
  cheese, softened
⅔ C. sugar
¼ tsp. salt
3 eggs
3 C. sour cream
2 tsp. lemon juice, fresh
2 Tbs. Maker's Mark
1 tsp. vanilla extract
2 Tbs. butter, melted

WAFER CRUST
1 (8½-ounce) box chocolate
  wafer cookies
¼ C. sugar
6 Tbs. butter, melted
10 pieces Maker's Mark Mint
  Julep Creme Candies,
  chopped

- Preheat oven to 350°.
- Beat cream cheese, sugar, salt and eggs in mixer at high speed until smooth. Add sour cream, lemon juice, bourbon, vanilla and butter; mix thoroughly.
- Pour filling into crust and bake in middle of oven for 45 minutes. Turn off oven, prop oven door open slightly and allow to rest 1 hour. Cool and refrigerate overnight.
- Prepare *Wafer Crust* by grinding cookies into fine crumbs. Add sugar; mix. Pour butter over crumbs and toss with fork to moisten evenly. Gently press crumbs evenly over bottom of 9-inch springform pan. (Reserve extra crumbs for garnishing top of cake.)
- Serve cheesecake in small slices garnished with wafer crumbs and chopped candies.

BOURBONESE DESSERT

Serves 6

"This is very sweet and small servings are perfect. Caramelized milk dessert can also be served over angel food cake as a topping."

1 (14-ounce) can condensed
  milk
2 egg whites, stiffly beaten
3 Tbs. Maker's Mark
Whipped cream, as garnish

- Remove paper from milk can. Place can in saucepan and cover completely with water. Boil at least 3 hours. (Be sure to keep can covered with water at all times. If it boils dry, it will explode.)
- Open can and pour caramelized milk over stiffly beaten egg whites; gently blend. If egg whites start to get lumpy, use an electric mixer and beat until smooth. While mixing hot caramelized milk with egg whites, add bourbon, a little at a time.
- Serve immediately in individual dessert dishes, 4 tablespoons to a serving. Garnish with whipped cream, if desired.

MAKER'S PARADISE CREAM CAKE

Serves 24

*"One of the most extraordinary desserts you'll ever eat — and it begins
with Maker's Paradise Cream, homemade in your kitchen."*

2 C. cake flour

2 tsp. baking powder

½ tsp. salt

½ C. butter

2 C. sugar

2 eggs

4 (1-ounce) squares unsweetened chocolate, melted

1 tsp. vanilla

1 C. Maker's Paradise Cream
(recipe on p. 105)

½ C. milk

1 C. walnuts, chopped

MAKER'S PARADISE CREAM
FROSTING

1 (8-ounce) pkg. cream cheese,
softened

4 C. confectioners' sugar

Maker's Paradise Cream

½ C. walnuts, chopped

- Preheat oven to 350° and grease 2 (8-inch) cake pans.

- Sift together first three ingredients. Cream butter and sugar in bowl; add eggs, one at a time, beating well. Mix in melted chocolate and vanilla.

- Add milk to Maker's Paradise Cream; combine flour mixture and Paradise Cream mixture with creamed mixture, beating well after each addition. Stir in walnuts.

- Pour into 2 (8-inch) pans and bake at 350° for 30 minutes or until done.

- Prepare *Maker's Paradise Cream Frosting* by creaming cream cheese and confectioners' sugar. Add small amount of Paradise Cream to reach spreading consistency. Fold in nuts.

- With serrated knife cut each cake horizontally into 2 layers. Frost between each layer and stack to make a four-layer cake; also frost top and sides.

- Serve by slicing in thin pieces — because it's so rich.

BOURBON AND LIME SAUCED MELON BALLS

Serves 8

*"Always a hit and can be served as an appetizer, salad,
accompaniment or dessert."*

⅔ C. granulated sugar

⅓ C. water

3 Tbs. lime juice

3 Tbs. orange juice

½ C. Maker's Mark

1½ C. cantaloupe balls

1½ C. honeydew melon balls

1½ C. watermelon balls

Mint, for garnish

- Cut all melon balls and set aside.

- Mix sugar and water in saucepan; bring to a boil. Turn back to simmer for 5 minutes; after cooking, let cool.

- Stir in lime juice, orange juice and bourbon. Pour over melon balls and chill, covered, for several hours.

- Garnish with mint before serving.

ANGEL ORANGE DELIGHT

Serves 12

"Add a surprise to this dessert by garnishing with finely chopped Maker's Mark Bourbon Chocolates — everyone loves it."

1 (6-ounce) can unsweetened frozen orange juice concentrate

1 (14-ounce) can sweetened condensed milk

1 (8-ounce) container whipped topping

3 small cans mandarin oranges, drained

CHOCOLATE CRUST

2 C. graham crumbs

3 Tbs. sugar

2 Tbs. unsweetened cocoa powder

6 Tbs. butter, softened

2 Tbs. Maker's Mark

- Prepare crust and press into bottom of glass soufflé bowl. Make decorative scallop pattern in crust by using back of small spoon.

- Make filling by blending orange juice with milk. Fold in whipped topping and oranges; do not beat.

- Pour mixture over prepared crust and garnish with reserved crumbs.

- Refrigerate or freeze until ready to serve.

- Prepare *Chocolate Crust* by combining graham cracker crumbs, sugar and cocoa powder; mix thoroughly. Blend in butter until mixture looks like coarse meal; sprinkle with bourbon. Spoon into dish; pat evenly into bottom and use spoon to make decorative pattern. Cover with foil and freeze for at least 10 minutes before filling.

SAMUELS' PARFAIT

Serves 6

"The parfaits may be made in advance and put in freezer. I always add extra warmed sauce to freezer parfait and whipped cream just before serving."

1 pt. vanilla ice cream

1 pt. strawberry ice cream

1 pt. pistachio ice cream

PARFAIT SAUCE

½ C. butter

1 C. sugar

1 egg, beaten

¼ C. Maker's Mark

1 tsp. instant coffee granules

Whipped cream, for garnish

- Prepare *Parfait Sauce* by melting butter in saucepan; stir in sugar. Cook over medium heat, stirring constantly, until sugar melts. Combine egg, bourbon and coffee granules; stir into sugar mixture. Cook over low heat, stirring, for 2 minutes; cool slightly.

- Assemble parfaits by placing scoops of ice cream in glasses. Spoon warmed sauce over ice cream, top with whipped cream and serve immediately or freeze for later.

SENATOR'S CHOCOLATE DESSERT

Serves 12

"A dessert that pleases everyone, especially men. Make up to a week in advance for less hassle on party day."

1 C. butter, softened
1½ C. sugar
1 Tbs. Maker's Mark
3 squares unsweetened
  chocolate, melted
4 eggs
1 C. whipping cream, stiffly
  beaten and sweetened,
  (if desired)

DESSERT CRUST

1 C. flour
½ C. brown sugar, packed
½ C. butter
½ C. pecans, chopped

- Prepare dessert crust and chill.

- Cream sugar and butter together. Add bourbon and melted chocolate.

- Beat in eggs, one at a time, beating 5 minutes between each egg addition.

- Pour mixture over crust and place in freezer for 30 minutes. Remove and spread with whipped cream.

- Cover tightly and store in freezer until ready to serve.

- Prepare *Dessert Crust* by combining all ingredients and spread on 2 jelly-roll pans. Bake at 350° for 12 minutes, or until golden, stirring occasionally. Immediately turn out onto cool cookie sheets and break into fine crumbs. Pat loosely into 9x13-inch pan; chill until firm.

SILVER PARTY NOG

Serves 24

"This drink is made without heavy cream — evaporated milk is used instead."

12 whole eggs
1 lb. confectioners' sugar
½ tsp. salt
4 Tbs. vanilla extract
8 C. evaporated milk
3 C. water
4 C. Maker's Mark
Nutmeg, for garnish

- Beat eggs until light in color; gradually beat in sugar, salt and vanilla.

- Stir in evaporated milk that has been diluted with 3 cups water.

- Blend bourbon in slowly. Cover nog and allow to ripen in refrigerator for 24 hours. Stir well before filling punch bowl.

- Chill silver punch bowl by leaving on cold porch an hour before filling with nog. Dust mixture with nutmeg before serving.

MINI BAKED ALASKAS — KENTUCKY STYLE *Serves 8*

"This dessert is always fun to serve — so easy, yet so elegant."

8 dessert sponge cakes, or any
   cake cut into 4-inch rounds
8 scoops ice cream (any flavor)
6-8 Tbs. Maker's Mark
3 egg whites
6 Tbs. confectioners' sugar

- Preheat oven to 475°.

- Arrange sponge cakes on layer of foil on cookie sheet. Sprinkle teaspoon of bourbon on each individual cake. Place medium size scoop of ice cream on each cake. With thumb, make small depression in each scoop and fill with bourbon; freeze.

- Beat egg whites until soft peaks form; gradually add sugar, beating until stiff and glossy. Cover ice cream and cake completely with meringue, sealing all around bottoms. Alaskas may be frozen at this point if needed for later use.

- Bake Alaskas about 5 minutes, or until meringue is lightly browned.

- Serve at once, flaming with additional bourbon, if desired.

Derby Oaks Branch   ■ *Family Celebrations*   ■ *Holiday and Party Fare*

I f you appreciate the painstaking way a craftsman goes about his trade and the methodical way he carries out every step to make the best, you may feel right at home with Maker's Mark.

Today, Bill Samuels, Jr., is still making Maker's Mark whisky… still handcrafting it the same slow, careful way his father started making it in 1953.

That's why Maker's Mark still produces only 38 barrels a day, compared to 1,300 barrels a day by the nation's largest distiller. Perhaps that's also why, in competitions from San Francisco to London, Maker's Mark continues to be judged the best bourbon in the world.

The next time you're near Loretto, Kentucky, stop by and say hello. Our people are always glad to see visitors, and they'll make you feel right at home as you tour Maker's Mark, the oldest continuously operating distillery in the country… and now a national landmark.

And remember, we only make 38 barrels a day. So you may have to search to find it. Most people think it's worth the trouble because Maker's Mark has "that special touch".

Opposite side photo: Country Bourbon Ham with Celebration Corn and Squash Casserole

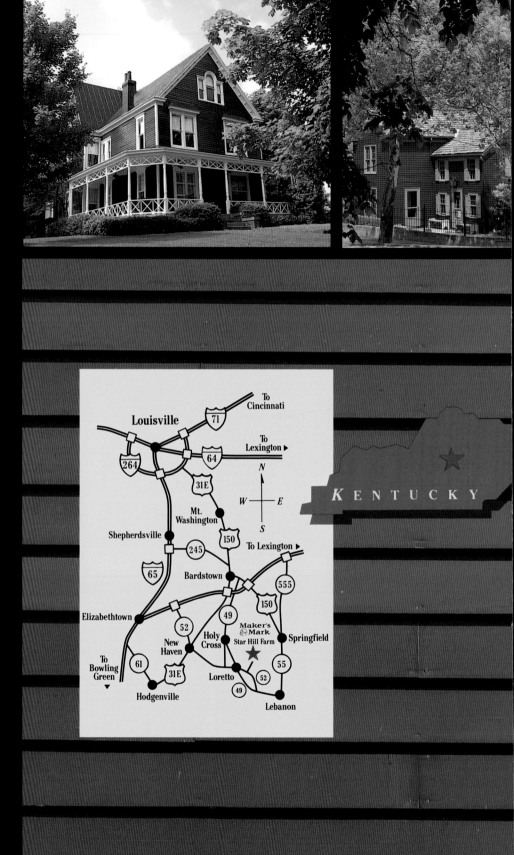

DERBY OAKS BRUNCH

"In Kentucky there's a belief that nothing goes together better than bourbon and horseracing. So at Maker's Mark, the Kentucky Derby is reason to celebrate…it's the best of both worlds. This menu has been served for the Samuels' Derby Brunch for many years. Don't be surprised if someday it turns up to be as famous as the Derby and Maker's Mark. Please note that the Country Ham recipe is presented in another Maker's Menu."

◆ ◆ ◆ ◆ ◆

Ambrosia   Baked Apples

Baked Country Ham

Corn Pudding   Vegetable Medley

Cheese Grits

Apple Spice Cake with Oaks Bourbon Sauce

Pecan Bourbon Pie

◆ ◆ ◆ ◆ ◆

OAKS AMBROSIA   *Serves 6*

"A special dish from the heavens."

1 (20-ounce) can chunk
   pineapple in juice
1 (11-ounce) can mandarin
   orange segments
1 C. seedless grapes
1 C. miniature marshmallows
1 C. flaked coconut
½ C. walnuts, broken into
   pieces
¾ C. sour cream or vanilla
   yogurt
1 Tbs. granulated sugar

- Drain pineapple and oranges; combine with next 4 ingredients.

- Mix sour cream and sugar; stir into fruit mixture.

- Chill and serve; recipe can easily be doubled.

OAKS BAKED APPLES

Serves 6

"This can be served as a hot salad, an accompaniment to any meat, or as a dessert — what an adaptable dish."

½ C. packed brown sugar
¼ C. granulated sugar
1 tsp. cinnamon
½ tsp. nutmeg
⅛ tsp. salt
1 (20-ounce) can sliced pie apples
1 Tbs. butter, melted
2 Tbs. Maker's Mark

- Mix first 5 ingredients together. Combine with pie slices, mixing thoroughly. Pour into 9x13-inch baking dish.
- Mix butter and bourbon; drizzle over apple casserole.
- Bake in 300° oven about 30 minutes or until bubbly.

OAKS CORN PUDDING

Serves 6

"Corn pudding — a true southern delicacy — is usually served and really expected at Derby gatherings."

7 Tbs. flour
4 Tbs. sugar or less, if desired
1 tsp. salt
2 C. whole kernel corn
2 C. cream style corn
4 eggs, well beaten
¼ tsp. nutmeg
2 Tbs. butter
3 C. milk (can use 1½ C. evaporated milk and 1½ C. whole milk)

- Preheat oven to 325° and grease a 2-quart dish.
- Combine flour, sugar and salt; add kernel corn and stir coating kernels. Add creamed corn to mixture.
- Blend eggs, nutmeg and butter into mixture. Add milk, mix thoroughly and pour into greased casserole dish.
- Bake at 325° for 45 – 60 minutes or until middle of casserole is set.
- *Hint*—Please double recipe to serve 12. Corn pudding can be baked in advance of serving and frozen until needed. Initial baking should be about 40 minutes or longer if recipe is doubled; freeze, thaw and reheat in oven over a pan of steaming water. (I freeze mine in large metal 9x13-inch pans.)

OAKS VEGETABLE MEDLEY

Serves 12

"A pretty salad — serve in large crystal bowl."

1 large head cauliflower,
  broken into flowerets
1 (10-ounce) pkg. frozen peas,
  thawed
1 C. celery, chopped
½ – 1 C. carrots, grated
1 small red onion, chopped
1 small white onion, chopped
1 bunch broccoli, cut into
  flowerets

DRESSING
2 C. mayonnaise
1⅓ C. salad oil
1⅓ C. white vinegar
1 C. sugar
2 tsp. salt
2 tsp. pepper

- Mix first 6 ingredients together and stir.
- Combine *Dressing* ingredients and blend well.
- Add broccoli last and pour *Dressing* over all vegetables.
- Refrigerate overnight; next day, stir several times to blend flavors.

OAKS CHEESE GRITS

Serves 6

"This dish is also a favorite at 'pot-luck' suppers."

2 C. boiling water
1⅓ C. instant grits
1½ C. shredded cheddar
  cheese
¼ C. grated parmesan cheese
2 eggs, well beaten
2 Tbs. freeze dried chives
Paprika, for garnish

- Preheat oven to 350° and grease an 8x12-inch baking dish.
- Pour boiling water over grits, stirring until blended. Add cheeses, mixing thoroughly, until all cheeses are melted. Blend in eggs and chives; sprinkle paprika on top.
- Pour into greased baking dish and bake 40 minutes or until knife inserted into center comes out clean.
- Recipe can be doubled to serve 12.

OAKS APPLE SPICE CAKE WITH OAKS BOURBON SAUCE *Serves 12*

*"This cake freezes well — prepare several days before your party
so flavors can mellow."*

3 C. flour

2 C. sugar

1½ tsp. baking soda

1 tsp. each of nutmeg, cinnamon, allspice and salt

2 eggs, well beaten

1 C. cooking oil

1 (21-ounce) can apple pie filling

2 Tbs. Maker's Mark

1 C. nuts, chopped

OAKS BOURBON SAUCE

½ C. brown sugar

1 tsp. cornstarch

⅛ tsp. salt

1 C. boiling water

2 Tbs. butter

½ tsp. vanilla extract

2 Tbs. Maker's Mark

- Preheat oven to 300° and grease a 9x13-inch pan.

- Blend first 7 dry ingredients together. Add eggs, oil, apple pie filling and bourbon, mixing well.

- Gently blend in nuts and pour into 9x13-inch pan. Bake at 300° for 45-55 minutes or until toothpick inserted comes out relatively clean.

- Prepare *Oaks Bourbon Sauce* by combining all dry ingredients, mixing well. Add water and cook 5 minutes, stirring often or until thickened. Remove from heat; add butter, vanilla and bourbon, mixing thoroughly. Serve warm over cake.

OAKS PECAN BOURBON PIE *Serves 6*

"This pie can be made into 6 small tarts so there's no pie to slice, just serve."

1 (9-inch) unbaked pie shell

5½ Tbs. butter

½ C. packed dark brown sugar

3 large eggs

¼ tsp. salt

1 C. dark corn syrup

2 Tbs. Maker's Mark

1 C. pecans, chopped

1 Tbs. flour

Pecan halves, for garnish

- Preheat oven to 350°; prepare pie shell or thaw frozen shell.

- Cream butter; add brown sugar slowly beating constantly until all sugar is absorbed and mixture is fluffy.

- Add eggs (one at a time) beating well after each addition. Add salt, corn syrup and bourbon.

- Toss pecans in flour and fold into filling. Pour mixture into unbaked crust and bake at 350° for 35-40 minutes or until filling is firm. (Pie may be decorated with pecan halves the last 5 minutes of baking.)

- Garnish with whipped cream.

M · E · N · U

SPRING FAMILY DINNER

This dinner can be served anytime during the year, but spring is always a fun time to get together. Decorate your table with fresh spring yard flowers around the traditional Lamb Cake. The menu is full of surprises that your family will love — include an Easter Egg Hunt for an added surprise.

◆ ◆ ◆ ◆ ◆

Spiced Pear Salad

Country Bourbon Ham

Orange Mint Peas   Oven Tomatoes

Celebration Corn and Squash Casserole

Miracle Potato Rolls

Lamb Mold Cake

◆ ◆ ◆ ◆ ◆

SPICED PEAR SALAD   Serves 8

"Spiced pears and sauce can be made 1-2 days in advance — assemble salad just before serving."

½ C. packed brown sugar
3 Tbs. Maker's Mark
1 Tbs. lemon juice
¼ tsp. each ground cinnamon
    and nutmeg
⅛ tsp. ground cloves
1 (29-ounce) can pear halves,
    drained and ¼ C. juice
    reserved
4 ounces cream cheese
¼ C. nuts, chopped
8 lettuce leaves

■ Combine first 6 ingredients; cook on medium high until boiling, stirring constantly.

■ Add pear halves, stirring to coat. Cook until pears are thoroughly heated; refrigerate spiced pears until chilled.

■ Cut cream cheese into eight pieces. Shape into balls; roll in nuts.

■ Prepare each serving by placing pear half on lettuce leaf. Spoon on sauce and place cheeseball in hollow of each pear half.

COUNTRY BOURBON HAM

"A Kentucky 'sugar-cured' country ham plays an important part in entertaining at any time of the year. The ham keeps well under refrigeration for about 4 weeks. Ham does not freeze well, so reheat leftover ham in 350° oven for about 1 hour. Remaining ham will keep under refrigeration for another month. Slice ham only as you need it — it's always the standby meat at most family gatherings or holiday celebrations."

1 (14-15) lb. country ham
2 C. water

GLAZE
1 C. Maker's Mark
1 C. light brown sugar
Cloves, for garnish

- Soak ham, completely submerged in water, overnight. Drain water; scrub with stiff brush.
- Preheat oven to 500°.
- Place water in large roaster. Put ham in skin side up and cover. Cook in 500° oven for 1 minute per pound.
- Turn off oven for 2 hours. *Do not open oven!*
- Reheat oven to 500°; when oven has reached temperature, start timing and cook ham 1 minute per pound. Turn off heat and leave ham in oven for at least 6 hours without opening oven.
- Remove ham from cooking liquid; trim off skin and excess fat while still warm.
- Cut remaining fat ½-inch deep in diamond pattern. Combine bourbon and brown sugar. Brush glaze over ham and dot with cloves.
- Return ham to 300° oven to brown glaze for about 30 minutes. Do not cut ham until thoroughly cool and slice very thin.

ORANGE-MINT PEAS

"A surprising combination of flavors with delicious results."

2 (10-ounce each) pkgs.
   frozen peas
5 Tbs. fresh orange juice
2 tsp. each of lemon juice and
   sugar
2 Tbs. fresh crushed mint
2 Tbs. butter
½ tsp. salt
¼ tsp. white pepper
Whole mint leaves and fresh
   slivers of orange peel for
   garnish

- Cook peas according to package directions; do not overcook. Drain, add orange juice, lemon juice, sugar and mint; stir to blend.
- Add butter, salt and pepper. Serve garnished with whole mint leaves and fresh slivers of orange peel.

OVEN TOMATOES

"The perfect addition of color and flavor to any meal."

10 medium tomatoes,
   cut in half
½ C. butter
2 tsp. seasoned salt
1½ tsp. garlic powder
1½ tsp. dill weed
1½ C. cornflake crumbs

- Combine all ingredients except tomatoes. Spread mixture over cut side of tomatoes and place in a 9x13-inch baking dish; refrigerate overnight.
- Next day, bake at 300° for 35 minutes or until tomatoes are thoroughly heated.
- Tomatoes are best when served hot.

CELEBRATION CORN AND SQUASH CASSEROLE

Serves 8

"A new way to prepare the old standby vegetable — corn."

1½ lbs. summer squash, thinly
   sliced
1 large red onion, thinly sliced
2 eggs, well beaten
1 C. corn, well drained
1 C. evaporated milk
1 tsp. baking powder
1 C. unseasoned bread crumbs
1 C. cheddar cheese, grated
Salt and pepper to taste
2 Tbs. butter

- Preheat oven to 350° and grease a 2-quart casserole.
- Cover squash and onion with water in a saucepan and cook over high heat until tender; drain.
- Stir in remaining ingredients and blend evenly together.
- Pour corn and squash mixture into greased casserole dish. Dot top of casserole with butter and bake for 1 hour, or until golden brown.

MIRACLE POTATO ROLLS

Yields 4 dozen

"These rolls are ready to bake whenever you need them. Homemade rolls have never been so easy and delicious."

⅔ C. margarine
⅔ C. sugar
1 tsp. salt
1 C. mashed potatoes,
   unseasoned
2 C. hot potato water, drained
1 pkg. yeast
2 eggs, beaten
7 C. all-purpose flour

- Mix together first 5 ingredients, blending well; cool mixture to lukewarm.
- Add yeast, eggs and flour; stir until all ingredients are thoroughly mixed. Place mixture in well-greased bowl; cover and refrigerate for 1 hour.
- You can now make rolls. Roll dough out on floured surface and shape into favorite variety of rolls. (Punch dough down every 8–10 hours if there is dough leftover.) These rolls are especially good when shaped into crescents.
- Place rolls on greased pan and bake at 375° for 10 minutes or until brown.

"Bake in a heavy iron lamb mold which can be found at an antique shop or gourmet food store. This cake makes a wonderful birthday cake for any age celebrity — a tradition you might like to begin."

½ C. butter
1½ C. sugar
2½ C. cake flour, sifted
2 tsp. baking powder
¼ tsp. salt
¾ C. milk
1 tsp. vanilla extract
⅛ tsp. salt (additional)
4 egg whites
1 Tbs. flour (additional)
2 Tbs. shortening (additional)

WHIPPED CREAM ICING

1 envelope gelatin (unflavored)
2 Tbs. Maker's Mark
2 C. heavy cream
¼ C. sugar

■ Preheat oven to 350°.

■ Cream butter, add sifted sugar gradually. Blend until fluffy.

■ Sift flour with baking powder and salt; add to batter mixture alternately with milk. Add vanilla.

■ Add ⅛ tsp. salt to egg whites and beat until stiff. Fold beaten egg whites gently into cake batter.

■ Grease heavy lamb mold sections with mixture of 1 tablespoon flour and 2 tablespoons shortening. Brush over both inside sections of mold. Turn batter into face side of mold, filling it level. Place top section of mold on top.

■ Bake at 350° for 50–55 minutes. Remove mold from oven, lift off top mold, and let cool before removing cake from mold. Frost with favorite icing or *Whipped Cream Icing*. Press grated coconut on frosting for wool effect.

■ Prepare *Whipped Cream Icing* by dissolving gelatin with Maker's Mark; stir in cream and sugar. Chill for 30 minutes.

■ Whip until heavy peaks form. This frosting will hold on cake for a day or two. Garnish with coconut.

HOLIDAY BRUNCH

This brunch is perfect for entertaining during the busy holidays or anytime during the year. It's a casual way of gathering a small or large group of friends, and it doesn't require lots of preparation. I've included several dishes which will make an impressive table — but you may wish to select only a few dishes for lighter entertaining. Try having a brunch before an afternoon sports event — entertaining has never been so easy.

◆ ◆ ◆ ◆ ◆

Punch Bowl Juleps

Holiday Brunch Casserole

Ham 'n Biscuits   Fancy Meatballs

Fruit Bowl with Strawberry Sauce

Baked Mushrooms   Smoked Oyster Tomatoes

Kentucky Sweet Breads

◆ ◆ ◆ ◆ ◆

PUNCH BOWL JULEPS   *Yields ½ gallon*

"Juleps for a crowd."

1 C. fresh mint leaves
¼ lb. sugar
3 oranges
3 lemons
3 limes
1 qt. Maker's Mark
1 qt. ginger ale

- Crush mint leaves and combine with sugar.
- Cut fruits in half, squeeze for juice and combine with mint mixture — including also 1 rind from each different fruit. Mix well and chill.
- When ready to serve, place mint mixture, whisky and ginger ale in punch bowl over chunk of ice; garnish with mint leaves and enjoy.

HOLIDAY BRUNCH CASSEROLE

Serves 12

"This moist casserole can be cooked, frozen and then reheated when needed."

2 lbs. sausage
10 slices white bread
1 lb. cheddar cheese, grated
8 eggs, well beaten
2½ C. milk
¼ tsp. dry mustard
1 C. cream of celery soup
½ tsp. salt
¼ tsp. pepper
Paprika, for garnish

- Brown sausage till crumbly and drain well.
- Trim crusts from bread and cut into cubes.
- Layer sausage, bread and grated cheese twice (in order given) in greased 9x13-inch casserole. (You will have 6 layers total — 2 layers of each.)
- Blend eggs, milk, mustard, soup, salt and pepper in blender. Pour over layered casserole and bake in 350° oven for 1 hour. (Place casserole in shallow pan of water during cooking.)
- Sprinkle with paprika just before serving.

HAM 'N BISCUITS

Serves 8

"Always the perfect way to serve Kentucky Country Ham — these biscuits are reminiscent of those famed beaten biscuits."

½ C. plus 2 Tbs. milk
2 Tbs. butter
1¾ C. flour
⅛ tsp. salt

- Preheat oven to 400° and grease baking sheet.
- Combine milk and butter in saucepan over low heat until butter is melted.
- Sift flour and salt into bowl and pour milky butter gradually into it. Stir well until mixture becomes soft dough. Roll out very thin on well-floured board and cut into 2-inch rounds, using fluted cookie cutter.
- Prick each round several times with fork and place biscuits pricked side down on well-greased baking sheet. Bake 5 minutes, then turn and bake for another 5 minutes. Biscuits should be lightly colored but not brown.
- Cool on wire rack; store in air tight container.
- Serve with thinly sliced baked Kentucky ham.

FANCY MEATBALLS

Yields 4 dozen

"A spirited side dish that adds spice to any occasion."

2 beaten eggs
⅓ C. dry bread crumbs, fine
1 (2¼-ounce) can deviled ham
½ tsp. salt
⅛ tsp. pepper
1 lb. lean ground beef
1 (22-ounce) can mincemeat
   pie filling
¼ C. apple juice
3 Tbs. Maker's Mark

- Combine eggs, bread crumbs, ham, salt and pepper; add ground beef and mix well. Shape into meatballs.
- Place in shallow baking pan. Bake at 375° until done, 12–14 minutes. Cool, remove from pan, cover and chill.
- Prepare sauce by combining pie filling, apple juice and bourbon. Heat till bubbly; add meatballs and heat thoroughly.
- Serve in chafing dish. Keep warm, adding additional apple juice if mixture becomes too thick.

FRUIT BOWL WITH STRAWBERRY SAUCE

Yields 1½ cups

"Cut up an assortment of fresh fruit and serve in individual crystal bowls with special STRAWBERRY SAUCE for loads of compliments."

1 (10-ounce) pkg. frozen
   strawberry slices
½ C. red pepper jelly
2 Tbs. cornstarch
2 Tbs. Maker's Mark

- Defrost strawberries on High in microwave; mash them with fork.
- Add jelly, cover and microwave on High until boiling.
- Mix cornstarch with bourbon; add to hot strawberries; stirring well. Cover and microwave about 2 more minutes or until thickened.
- Serve over fresh pineapple, kiwi, strawberries and bananas or any fruit combination.

BAKED MUSHROOMS

Serves 8

"Serve in chafing dish to keep warm throughout meal."

2 lbs. fresh mushrooms
1 medium onion, sliced
½ C. margarine
1½ C. sour cream
2 Tbs. sherry
½ tsp. salt
¼ tsp. pepper

- Wash mushrooms; halve mushrooms if extra large.
- Sauté onion in melted margarine until limp. Add mushrooms, cover and cook slowly 5 minutes.
- Add cream, sherry and seasonings. Simmer until thoroughly heated.

SMOKED OYSTER TOMATOES

Yields 40

"The simplest of appetizers for any party — but oh so good."

40 cherry tomatoes
1 (3-ounce) can smoked oysters

- Wash and remove stems from cherry tomatoes.
- Cut down through each tomato to within ½ inch of base; spread apart just enough to slip canned oyster inside each.
- Serve at room temperature.

KENTUCKY SWEET BREADS

Yields 4 dozen

"Batter must be baked immediately or butter will settle and breads will be tough. Cut recipe in half or quarters, according to number of pans available."

1 C. sifted flour
¼ tsp. salt
4 eggs
1 Tbs. Maker's Mark
1 tsp. vanilla
⅔ C. sugar
½ C. butter, melted and cooled
Confectioners' sugar

BOURBONED CREAM
CHEESE
2 (3-ounce each) pkgs. cream
    cheese, softened
3 Tbs. confectioners' sugar
2 Tbs. butter, softened
3 Tbs. Maker's Mark

- Preheat oven to 325° and grease small muffin pans or special Madeleine pans. Sift flour and salt together.
- Beat eggs, bourbon and vanilla until light and fluffy. Add sugar gradually, beating constantly, until mixture is thick and fluffy.
- Carefully fold in flour mixture; quickly fold in butter. Spoon into prepared pans immediately, filling ¾ full.
- Bake at once in 325° oven for 12–15 minutes, or until lightly browned. Cool in pans 2–3 minutes. Turn onto wire racks, shell side up to cool if using Madeleine pans.
- Just before serving, sprinkle with confectioners' sugar or serve with *Bourboned Cream Cheese*.
- Prepare *Bourboned Cream Cheese* by combining all ingredients in small bowl. Beat until smooth, chill and store in refrigerator 24 hours before serving.

M · E · N · U

VILLAGE BARBECUE

A barbecue always signals an easy way of entertaining in the South. This style of hospitality can be as simple or as elaborate as you wish. I've included tasty, but easy, recipes which can be partially prepared in advance. I've found that guests appreciate a relaxed host or hostess more than complicated preparations of food. So enjoy your own party — everyone else will, too. And it's OK to ask guests to help out with those very last minute preparations. Add your own special bread for a complete menu.

◆ ◆ ◆ ◆ ◆

Celebration Punch

Village Pork

Marinated Tomatoes   Surprise Corn on the Cob

Maker's Vanilla Ice Cream

The Highlands Shortbread

◆ ◆ ◆ ◆ ◆

CELEBRATION PUNCH   *Serves 16*

"A slushy punch that's refreshing on a warm afternoon. Refreeze any leftover punch and enjoy on another day."

1 (3-ounce) pkg. strawberry
   gelatin
1 C. sugar
1 qt. pineapple juice
1 (6-ounce) can frozen lemonade, thawed
1 qt. ginger ale

- Dissolve gelatin in 4 cups of hot water; add sugar, pineapple juice and thawed lemonade.
- Pour into large plastic container and freeze.
- Remove from freezer about 2 hours before serving and remove from container. Pour ginger ale over frozen gelatin mixture, allow to dissolve.
- Punch is best when served slushy.

VILLAGE PORK

"Barbecue meat for easy entertaining — the main course cooks while guests are enjoying the party."

4 lbs. pork tenderloin
¾ C. Maker's Mark
3 tsp. salt
6 Tbs. sugar
6 Tbs. soy sauce

- Cut pork tenderloin into 2 long strips. Mix bourbon, salt, sugar and soy sauce into paste and rub into meat. Allow to stand for 3 hours so flavor penetrates the meat.
- Barbecue or broil meat slowly for 1 hour or until tender.
- When cool, cut into thin slices, serve on small buns and top with *Maker's Mark Gourmet Sauce* – about 1 tablespoon to each serving.

MARINATED TOMATOES

"A make-ahead salad — this is a perfect accompaniment to any meal, but especially great for using all those abundant summertime tomatoes."

4 large tomatoes, sliced
⅓ C. olive oil
¼ C. red wine vinegar
2 tsp. parsley flakes
2 tsp. onions, chopped
1 tsp. each of Italian seasoning
    and salt
½ tsp. sugar
¼ tsp. garlic salt
¼ tsp. coarsely ground pepper

- Arrange tomato slices in shallow container.
- Combine remaining ingredients; mix well and pour over tomatoes.
- Cover and marinate in refrigerator several hours or overnight.
- Take out of refrigerator about 1 hour before serving — tomatoes are usually best served at room temperature.

SURPRISE CORN ON THE COB　　　*Yields 12 ears*

"This is a favorite with all age groups — serve as an appetizer instead of vegetable with the meal."

12 ears corn, with husks
½ C. butter, melted
1 Tbs. fresh parsley, chopped
1 Tbs. lemon juice
½ tsp. salt
¼ tsp. garlic powder

- Soak corn overnight in large kettle of water. Drain and remove silk carefully, preserving husks attached to base of corn ear.
- In small bowl combine butter, parsley, lemon juice, salt and garlic. Brush ears with mixture and replace husks so ear is entirely wrapped again.
- Place over glowing coals of grill and roast until tender, 20–30 minutes; turn every 10 minutes.
- *Hint*— Corn can be brushed with Maker's Mark Gourmet Sauce instead of butter mixture. This is quite a change from traditional corn on the cob but it's delicious — try it as an appetizer. Let guests devour it as soon as it's "off the grill." Hold corn by husks and eat as finger food.

MAKER'S VANILLA ICE CREAM　　　*Yields 3 quarts*

"Be sure to prepare custard in advance and chill in refrigerator for at least 4 hours or overnight before freezing ice cream."

2 C. sugar
3 Tbs. cornstarch
¼ tsp. salt
3 C. half-and-half or whole milk
4 eggs, slightly beaten
4 C. heavy cream, chilled
1 Tbs. vanilla extract
½ C. Maker's Mark

- Combine first 3 ingredients in top of double boiler and stir in half-and-half or milk. Cook over gently simmering water, stirring constantly, until mixture thickens and cornstarch is cooked.
- Blend a small amount of hot mixture into beaten eggs; return egg mixture to pan, cooking for 5–6 minutes longer, stirring constantly. Remove from heat and cool slightly.
- Stir in cream, vanilla and bourbon slowly. Refrigerate mixture until freezing time.
- Freeze in hand-crank or electric freezer, following instructions of freezer.
- Use above recipe to prepare *Peach Ice Cream* by increasing sugar to 2¼ cups. Reduce vanilla to 2 teaspoons and leave out bourbon. While custard is chilling, mash 2 cups fresh peaches and chill; add to custard mixture just before freezing.

THE HIGHLANDS SHORTBREAD   *Yields 12 cookies*

*"A simply perfect cookie to serve with fresh homemade ice cream
of any flavor."*

1¼ C. all-purpose flour
3 Tbs. cornstarch
¼ C. sugar
¼ C. butter, cut into pieces
2 Tbs. sugar, for garnish

■ Stir together flour, cornstarch and ¼ C. sugar in mixing bowl. Rub in butter with fingers until mixture is crumbly. Form mixture into ball and place in ungreased (9-inch) springform pan. Press out dough into an even layer.

■ With tines of fork, make line impressions around edge of dough; prick surface evenly with fork.

■ Bake in 325° oven for 40 minutes or until pale golden brown. Remove from oven and cut with sharp knife into 12 wedges while hot. Sprinkle entire shortbread with 1–2 tablespoons sugar.

■ Let cool completely; remove sides of pan and lift out cookies.

STAR SELECTIONS

TARTS & TEA CAKES

SWEET SPLURGES

CONFECTIONS

HAPPY ENDINGS

MAKER'S MENUS

GIVE A GIFT IN GOOD TASTE.

Order That Special Touch Cookbook for family and friends.

For information on Maker's Mark Distillery tours, the Maker's Mark Gift Gallery or where to find Maker's Mark in your area, contact:

**Maker's Mark Distillery
1-TST
Loretto, KY 40037
(502) 865-2881**

To order Maker's Mark Bourbon Chocolates or Mint Julep Cremes, contact:

**Ehrler's Candies
1-TST
1370 Belmar Drive
Louisville, KY 40213
Fast Phone Orders: 1-800-456-1945**

To order Maker's Mark Gourmet Sauce, contact:

**Bourbon Country Products, Inc.
1-TST
1726 Mellwood Avenue
Louisville, KY 40206
(502) 897-9699
FAX (502) 896-2231**

*For additional copies, please fill in and return this form to **That Special Touch**.*

☐ Please send me _____ copies of ***That Special Touch*** @ $39.95 each, plus postage, handling and applicable taxes.

Name _____

Address _____

City _____ State _____ Zip _____

☐ Please send ***That Special Touch*** to a friend @ $39.95 each, plus postage, handling and applicable taxes.

☐ Gift Message, if applicable:

_____

Ship To:

Name _____

Address _____

City _____ State _____ Zip _____

That Special Touch	**(Enter Total)**
$39.95 (Per Copy)	$_____
Postage/Handling	
$4.00 First Copy	$_____
Additional Copies	
$2.00 Each *(With same order)*	$_____
KY Residents add Sales	
Tax *(per book)* $2.00	$_____
Total (Check or Credit Card)	$_____

Charge to: ☐ Visa ☐ MasterCard

Expiration Date

Signature _____
(Required for all charge cards)

Quantity discounts are available. For more information, call ***That Special Touch,*** (606) 336-7749. All orders shipped promptly.

Mail to:

That Special Touch
**Sandra Davis
P.O. Box 427
Springfield, KY 40069**

**(606) 336-7749
FAX (606) 336-3960**